INVISIBLE

Available on AMAZON.com

INVISIBLE

Ephesians 6:12 (NLT)
> *"For we are not fighting against flesh – and – blood enemies, but against evil rulers and authorities of the unseen (INVISIBLE)world, against mighty powers in this dark world, and against evil spirits in the heavenly (INVISIBLE) places."*

J.C. Story

Opinions in this book are provided for information purposes only. Although the author has made every effort to ensure that the information in this book was correct at the time of first publication, the author does not assume and hereby disclaims any liability to any party for any loss, damage, or disruption caused by errors or omissions, whether such errors or omissions result from negligence, accident, or any other cause.

Copyright © 2022 by J.C. Story

All rights reserved. No part of this book may be reproduced or transmitted in any form or by any means, electronic or mechanical, including photocopying, recording, or any information storage and retrieval system, without permission in writing from the author.

ISBN: 978-0-578-96215-3

Printed in the United States of America   1 1 1 0 2 2

∞This paper meets the requirements of ANSI/NISO Z39.48-1992 (Permanence of Paper)

Author Photo by: Cassandra Carrigan
Other photos by: Jim Jernigan, Michael David Edwards, Mary Ann Sherman, and Peter Borsari

In Remembrance of Victor and Danna Hvolboll

40% of the Authors profits of this book will go directly to *OPERATION BLESSING UKRAINE.*
They have been in Ukraine for over 20 years and will continue to be there for all Ukrainian refugees. Please see their informational website for more information about what they do in Ukraine.

……………………………………………………..

OPERATION BLESSING UKRAINE CRISIS
977 Centerville Turnpike
Virginia Beach, Virginia 23463
1-800-730-2537
OB.ORG/CRISIS

Contents

INTRODUCTION ix

CHAPTER 1	GOD's Wi-Fi	1
CHAPTER 2	The Laws	13
CHAPTER 3	Waiting in Line to See GOD	27
CHAPTER 4	JESUS: World Renowned Attorney/Defender	35
CHAPTER 5	Gold Is Purified by Fire, Man Is Purified by Gold	43
CHAPTER 6	Finish Your Game	53
CHAPTER 7	Your Real Enemy, There's Only One!	59
CHAPTER 8	Always Be Alert and of Sober Mind	93
CHAPTER 9	Invisible Music	101
CHAPTER 10	The Story of lucifer, satan the hacker	117
CHAPTER 11	STOP—BE STILL	135
CHAPTER 12	GOD's Great Beauty	155

WARNINGS FOR NEW CHRISTIANS 163
MOVIES EVERY NEW CHRISTIAN MUST SEE ... 169
WEEKLY SHOWS TO WATCH 173
MUST-READ BOOKS 175
DIRECTION FOR LIFE'S CHALLENGE'S 177

CLOSING BIBLE VERSE *183*
ACKNOWLEDGMENTS *187*

Introduction

The only introduction to this book would be the theme song of my life:

"It's a Jungle Out There" (2003)
By Randy Newman

It really is a Jungle Out There and this book can help tremendously!

CHAPTER 1

GOD'S WI-FI

The most powerful things in the world and the universe are all invisible; oxygen, carbon monoxide/dioxide, gravity, the wind, and aerodynamics—just to name a few. All invisible and all control the entire world around us. Like the wind, you cannot see it, however you most certainly can see the effects in hurricanes, tornadoes, power/electricity (via wind turbines), etc. That's how GOD/JESUS exist, HE has no origin, and you cannot see HIM, yet we are surrounded by HIS effects.

There are invisible powers all around us: in the aforementioned, and in the form of invisible radio waves, satellite signals, over-the-air digital TV, radio stations, etc., and last but not least, Wi-Fi. Our world and the entire earth is controlled and run by an astounding amount of invisible information, knowledge, and power—knowledge is power. There are so many different invisible signals just streaming through the air, all fighting for us to hook-up with them. All the different invisible satellite signals want us to connect with them. Then there is invisible streaming TV of all kinds and cellular phone companies also all trying to get us to request their invisible connections. I could go on, but you get the point. Just think about it, all the information of the entire world streaming through the air, all around us, 24/7! You don't feel it or see it but when you turn on the Wi-Fi, the power you have at your fingertips, incredible! Those facts—my friend—are oh so incredible, and true as the word "truth" itself. With Wi-Fi, you turn your computer on and choose which signal you will connect with. Our being (body, soul, and mind) can be compared with the computer, cellular phone, smart device, radio, satellite, T.V., etc. There is a component within each, which is built exclusively to receive invisible signals, likewise our being/souls have a built-in receiver as well. Both our being/soul and the aforementioned devices are built to receive invisible information which is streaming all around us through the air.

    Here is the situation though, if we do not make a conscious decision to connect our computer or device to a specific signal, it is impossible to receive all that invisible information and power streaming all around us in the air. Just because we are not connected to Wi-Fi does not mean that the information of the entire world is not out there in the air, all around us, 24/7, correct? I mean the internet is always out there invisible, in the air whether we believe it or not, nonetheless, it still exists—just like GOD/JESUS. The same is true of course with our being/souls. Our being/souls have a built-in receiver.

    There is wisdom, knowledge, love, good, and evil power streaming all around us in the spiritual form just like Wi-Fi, satellite, radio wave signals, etc. Just because someone does not believe it is there, that does not stop it from being there or existing just like Wi-Fi. Most people don't think about that very real reality. Nonetheless, believe it or not, that is in fact the situation. All invisible, all around us, massive information and power! Amazing! If you believe in and depend upon this invisible Wi-Fi around the clock, and you do most certainly believe in it, then why is it such a stretch to know that GOD/JESUS is out there in existence as well? All that powerful knowledge, all around us, just waiting for beings/souls to log-in and choose who they will connect with. What cell phone, internet, or satellite company will you choose? What spiritual Wi-Fi will you choose, GOD/JESUS or satan?

There are also destructive signals out there in the spiritual Wi-Fi realm. There are viruses and hackers and any number of bad and evil signals you can accidentally connect with if you are not vigilant.

So here are the basics of the situation, every day when you get on Wi-Fi you have either set your computer or device to receive a certain Wi-Fi signal, or you may go to select a new signal. Either way, you have made a daily choice to be connected to a certain signal, right? Now, in that same way, your soul is a receiver. Therefore, you must make a conscious decision every day to connect with a certain spiritual Wi-Fi.

Understand that there are two different spiritual companies wanting you to connect with them. There's good, and there is evil. In the same way you have "free will" to choose your internet's Wi-Fi or cellular phone company, you, too, have "free will" to choose your spiritual Wi-Fi company. Make no mistake, if you think you are going to go about life without a thought of your spiritual Wi-Fi—if you do not make an intentionally conscious choice of connection—one will be made for you. For those who pay no attention to their spiritual receiver, because people do not understand or acknowledge they have a receiver for spiritual Wi-Fi, there is this wide-open, unprotected receiver which anything (hackers, viruses, etc.) can connect with and completely take over. There are only two kinds of spiritual Wi-Fi companies out there: good (GOD/JESUS) and bad (satan). So, the best Wi-Fi companies would never want to force people to purchase their Wi-Fi. They try to advertise their best options, prices, protections, and whatever else they offer to get you to choose their company. Because good (GOD/JESUS) wants "free will" and true love, not prisoners or forced purchase of HIS Wi-Fi company. GOD/JESUS waits for us to come to HIM, like any good, reputable company or gentleman would. That's "free will," so that leaves good (GOD/JESUS) out of the equation unless or until you make an intentionally conscious choice to connect with good (GOD/JESUS). In comparison, GOD/JESUS puts out awesome advertisements all over the world to entice people to choose HIS spiritual Wi-Fi company. As I stated before, GOD/JESUS does not want prisoners or people being forced to receive HIS free Wi-Fi. "Free will" remember! Now you know the only other choice out there is bad (satan) Wi-Fi, and that's the crew which will be hacking into your unprotected receiver, reeking-havoc on your life!

This is how people end up doing things they thought they would never do. Ever been there before? I have—and that, my friend, is why our prisons are so full. Have you ever had a friend, or even yourself, that did something terrible which cannot be reversed or taken back? You absolutely cannot believe it and you cannot understand how it all happened. It's like you, or your friend, were just possessed while it was happening, then you woke up after all is said and done and it's unbelievably shocking to you. You, or your friend, got hacked a.k.a. possessed—hooked up to the wrong spiritual Wi-Fi.

Ever wonder why alcohol is called spirits? It is because way back in Biblical days people easily understood that demons or spirits would possess you if you drank too much. They knew that taking drugs or alcohol (spirits) would leave your very soul unprotected. It was common knowledge back then the damage a spirit could do to your life. For that reason, all mind-altering substances were called spirits, because taking too much was like baiting demons to take you over. Pouring spirits (alcohol/drugs) into your body compromises your soul's built-in protection just like pouring, say, water in a nice computer—it will compromise the computers built-in protection. A little usually won't do much damage but a lot can destroy the entire thing. Exactly like the computer, the more water (alcohol) poured inside the computer, the more damaged/compromised its built-in protections become. On the other hand, if you simply have a small spill (drink), a small amount won't do much damage. A small drink will not harm you; The Bible even says that, "a little wine for your digestion". It's excessive drinking/drugs that render a soul's built-in spiritual protection defenseless.

A good example is one of many incidents happening around the world, where a person has called one of those ride companies after having drank alcohol (spirits) excessively. Many have accidentally entered a random car, which they had assumed was their requested ride. They were then driven away and attacked or even murdered. This has happened many times around the world. This is classic evil spirits "M.O." These people were so filled with alcohol (spirits) that the spirits took them over and walked their bodies right to a car where other evil spirits were waiting within the driver who eventually attacked them. Neither one knew that their spiritual receiver/protection had been hacked, the random driver never imagined that a person would stagger to their car and jump in. None of this had been planned by the people themselves, however, the entire tragedy was planned by the spiritual hackers a.k.a. satan and his crew. This can happen to Christians just as easily as any non-believer, should one choose to drink excessively.

Back to your choices, there are only two—the good and the bad—one is a highly reputable company who has a long, long reputation for being on the up and up, you know what to expect from them—only "good" (GOD/JESUS). Likewise, with a company which is known for its scams and dishonesty throughout its entire history (satan and his crew), you know what to expect from them (satan-the-hacker): stealing, sending viruses, hacking into your being/soul, lying, and in general causing you to take the fall for satan's wrongdoing. That's the way satan lives. He's only happy when you are miserable. All satan sees when he looks at mankind is GOD/JESUS' creation that replaced him. All the adoration and love GOD/JESUS felt for Lucifer (now satan) was taken away and bestowed upon mankind, therefore, like the jilted ex, the devil/the hacker, absolutely hates your very existence. The devil only sees GOD/JESUS' love, hopes, and dreams in mankind, feelings which GOD/JESUS had had for Lucifer (now satan-the-hacker) before he decided to attempt a takeover in heaven (we will get into that later). Talk about biting the hand that feeds you.

We are all walking targets unless we choose wisely. You can just envision the devil at the moment when you've hit rock bottom, satan will be in his recliner, laughing hard at you. See the book *The Screw Tape Letter's* by C.S. Lewis (1898-1963) former atheist and writer of *The Chronicles of Narnia,* among other great books, he explains the lengths to which demons will go to destroy you.

Basically, NOT choosing GOD/JESUS' free Wi-Fi is like setting yourself up for the most invasive identity theft ever heard of! The master of all hackers is just hovering over you, waiting for any chance to slip into your receiver, like getting drunk, high, simply not paying attention, or not being connected to GOD/JESUS' protection plan (having your receiver open).

There was a doctor of psychiatry by the name of Dr. George G. Ritchie (1923-2007) General Practice and Psychiatry, I had read his book of an experience Dr. Ritchie had had during his service in World War II. He had been pronounced dead from double lumbar pneumonia prior to being shipped out. He said after having left his body he was standing at the entrance to a bar where people were sitting on stools drinking alcohol (spirits). He then said he was watching the people drinking at the bar. Dr. Ritchie said as they drank, these dark cloud-like human figures appeared behind them. As the people drank more and more, those dark spirits slowly moved closer to the people they were near. After the person had consumed so much alcohol that they had clearly lost control, the dark entities completely disappeared inside of the inebriated person. I will never forget that as long as I live, it sent chills down my spine, remembering how many times I had gotten so drunk or high. That one interview caused me to get serious about sobriety and I've been straight ever since.

Let me be crystal clear, GOD THE FATHER/CHRIST JESUS will never force you to connect with HIS spiritual Wi-Fi, never. GOD/JESUS will not trick you or hack you in order to give you access to HIS (absolutely free) great wisdom, blessings, power, protection, and love. GOD/JESUS is not going to beg and plead with you, nor force you to take advantage of HIS (all-free) protection, benefits package and Wi-Fi connection. GOD THE FATHER and JESUS THE CHRIST are no one's bitch! However, HE is ever longing relentlessly to love and help us.

On the other hand, what shyster, charlatan, evil entity would not take advantage of that which is of great value (your soul) and left unattended (not consciously connected)? If you do not connect your receiver daily with GOD/JESUS' Wi-Fi (HOLY SPIRIT), thinking you will just wing it, that's like owning the most expensive, top of the line, latest model computer or smartphone, etc., and then leaving it out on the sidewalk unattended! You can understand that it will be taken pretty damn quick.

If your soul has an open receiver/connection, then something will hook on to it just like that computer on the sidewalk. It will be taken and used for that evil entity's intentions. The unconscious connection is in-fact a theft of control, a hacking, and once downloaded you will be unknowingly filled with viruses just like hackers on the internet. Only with these viruses you can end up on drugs, destroying your family and/or marriage, in jail, or on death-row, maybe becoming an alcoholic, heroin addict, or in any number of extremely terrible situations; after which you and your friends are all saying, "how did that happen to such a good person? How did I ever get involved in this? How did this happen to me? I've always been a good person". Worst of all, just because you got hacked spiritually does not alleviate you of responsibility, you are still very much responsible because you did not check your spiritual Wi-Fi. It is your responsibility to govern your activities on this earth.

Being a good person or even a really good person has nothing to do with your spiritual Wi-Fi connection. There are plenty of great computers, smartphone's, etc., out there too, but just because the product is a good or great product does not protect it from hackers and viruses, or even pulling up child porn, or any number of wretched things. So being a great person will not protect you, just like being a great computer, smartphone, etc., top quality, will not stop that device from displaying horrible things from the Wi-Fi world from time to time. There are people all over the world right now fueling child sex trafficking and child pornography. They know it's wrong, yet they cannot seem to stop themselves, why? Because at some point or another, they got hacked and they have yet to discover it! Does anyone really grow-up dreaming of being a heroin addict, a drunk, a wife beater, murderer, or child molester?

GOD/JESUS says "No one is righteous—not even one" Romans 3:10 (NLT). We are all sinners (imperfect) and we can thank that jerk satan for that position. For this reason, GOD/JESUS provides awesome, amazing, incredibly powerful soul Wi-Fi streaming all around us full of love, protection and wisdom so that we have a way to escape the evil one. GOD/JESUS always, always provides another path to escape the evil one, so whenever you are facing a problem, "always do what GOD/JESUS would do and then leave the consequences to HIM" (famous words of Pastor Charles Stanley—a Ministry also en español). When we are facing a dilemma, GOD/JESUS is forever trying to guide us to the wisest way out. However, HE's not going to run behind you begging you to let HIM give you blessings, etc. forever, eventually HE will simply turn away until you call HIM. But satan, he's always running behind us, just waiting to trip us up or catch us off guard, our soul receiver open to any signal. Unlike GOD/JESUS, satan does not care how he obtains his patrons. He will take a soul any way he can, and taking souls without them noticing (until it's too late) is satan's specialty! Anything to hurt GOD/JESUS because satan was thrown to the earth as fast as lightning! Luke 10:18 (NLT) GOD/JESUS said, "I saw satan fall from heaven like lightning!" After all the hell satan has put me through, I find that verse absolutely hilarious!

Again, why does satan care? What does he get out of causing us to harm ourselves and each other? The devil understands just how much GOD/JESUS loves us human beings; by hurting us, satan hurts GOD/JESUS. The devil was kicked out of the number one position under GOD's SON JESUS and

THE HOLY SPIRIT. Kicked out of heaven, because satan wanted to take over GOD/JESUS' house which is heaven. What would you do if someone came into your home and tried to take it over, including your children, loved ones, everything and everyone? We would kick them out! As I stated before, satan fell to the earth at the speed of lightning, HUA, whappaw! Hilarious! Just think about all the times satan has hacked into your life and caused some major stuff to go down, and you will think satan falling like lightning is hilarious too.

In summary, let's review using a computer as the example:

GOD = Hard drive
JESUS = Wi-Fi transmitter
HOLY SPIRIT = Wi-Fi

And also using "the wind" as an example:

GOD = The Wind
JESUS = The Turbines (JESUS was created in human form by GOD just as man created the turbines)
HOLY GHOST = The power/energy/electricity that is produced by the turbines (of JESUS)

As a computer must have all three of the above, is as it is with GOD/JESUS and THE HOLY SPIRIT. Each of the three parts of a computer being separate parts, each having its own capabilities; however, when placed together they produce an invisible stream of all the world's knowledge. This is a good example of THE HOLY TRINITY, so are they three or are they one? The answer is they are ALL. Please understand that HOLY SPIRIT is also an entity unto itself just as GOD & JESUS are. For more about THE HOLY SPIRIT see Pat Robertson's book: ***The Power of The HOLY SPIRIT*** (original publish date 2022).

Little known fact: The creator of the original Wi-Fi signal-stream was Ms. Hedy Lamarr (1914-2000), American Austrian Inventor, Actress & Model. She was the most beautiful and intelligent woman of her time. There are several documentaries about her having figured out how to create Wi-Fi, it's an absolutely amazing story. And a side note: Hedy Lamarr was Jewish just like JESUS, so not only did GOD send The Bible through the Jewish people and HIMSELF/JESUS, but HE also sent Wi-Fi to Earth through the Jewish ancestry (among many, many other incredible inventions with which the world depends on today). Listen, today's so-called triple threats in show business have nothing on Hedy Lamarr, that kind of intelligence with that kind of overwhelming beauty is all but unheard of today! Thank you Ms. Hedy Lamarr! You were awesome! That's how GOD/JESUS rolls!

Please see: ***"TO LIFE"*** (2018) Documentary film by Gordon Robertson

2 Corinthians 4:18 (NIV)
> *"So, we fix our eyes not on what is seen, but on what is UNSEEN,*
> *Since what is seen is temporary, but what is UNSEEN is eternal"!*

CHAPTER 2

The Laws

There are rules and laws which accompany everything man-made and invisible. From our laws and regulations involving the Constitution, corporations, military, HOA's, etc. You name it and there are rules and laws to the use of it. The more valuable the privilege, the more strictly we must abide by its laws, or we lose our access and privileges. When it comes to cell phones, we are forced to abide by that company's rules or we lose our connection. With our driver's license, if we do not follow the traffic laws, we will lose our privilege of driving. In general, I think we can all agree if you do not abide by the laws, there will definitely be major problems. At your own home, for example, you would not allow some hellion to live in your house if they are constantly breaking the rules you have for living in your home. Would you put up with constant rule/law breaking inside your house? Would you allow a person to ransack your home daily and continue to still live with you? Why, then, do we expect GOD/JESUS to allow us to constantly destroy things, people, ourselves and break all HIS laws on HIS earth without repercussions? After all,

GOD/JESUS only wants us to enjoy and love each other and the world/home HE's provided for us.

Let's take this thought further, GOD/JESUS made all these universal laws and sciences—yes you heard me—GOD/JESUS created science, so it stands to reason that HE believes in it.

Look up Scientific Creationist Dr. Grady McMurtry of Creation World View Ministries.

Also see the series *Creation in the 21st Century* (David Rives)—a solid case for CHRIST JESUS using a combination of creation, Biblical astronomy and archaeology. (Description from IMDb.com)

What follows here are a few examples of invisible Universal Laws. There are invisible laws/rules that will cause death if not precisely followed. Flying a jet, for example, aerodynamics meaning the properties of a solid object regarding the manner in which air flows around it. A plane has the aerodynamics of a brick once the forward thrust is lost (Oxford Languages). Aerodynamics embody invisible laws that must not be broken, or you'll face death. If you do not follow the invisible laws of aerodynamics while flying a jet, you will probably not survive. Therefore, we have no problem, whatsoever, adhering to the invisible laws of aerodynamics, it is absolutely unthinkable to rebel against these invisible laws!

Same thing with a boat, hydrodynamics, the branch of science concerned with forces acting on or exerted by fluids (especially liquids) (Oxford Languages). If you do not follow the invisible laws of hydrodynamics while boating, for example, things could easily end in death. Again, there are thermodynamics—which is a GOD/JESUS made universal—

and physical science (just like all the others) which deals with the relations between heat and other forms of energy (such as mechanical, electrical, or chemical energy) and, by extension, of the relationships between all forms of energy (definition from Oxford Languages). All of the aforementioned invisible laws involve a mix of mechanical rules, human laws, and the natural GOD/JESUS created laws of the earth (air, water, chemical, etc.).

I am moving toward a point; the point is that just like all other invisible, powerful forces and their respective invisible laws, GOD/JESUS has HIS own set of rules (solely for our benefit). Nothing is without law, absolutely nothing and certainly not the most powerful of all the invisible powers, the creator GOD-HIMSELF! All of the aforementioned invisible powers cannot be enjoyed without the adherence of their coinciding laws and rules. You would not even consider flying a plane or driving a boat without incorporating and adhering to their respective invisible dynamic laws. Why, then, do we completely bypass GOD/JESUS' existence and HIS coinciding laws (which are only to protect us from ourselves)? GOD/JESUS is just as real as all of the above-mentioned invisible powers. Again, I state that the most powerful things in the world (oxygen, gravity, the wind, carbon dioxide, etc.) are the invisible ones! Once you really get a good grip on that complete depth and understanding, then you can clearly comprehend that it stands to reason, and is only common sense, that GOD/JESUS is really there—the wind alone with all its different powers proves that. Listen, we readily obey the laws of all those other invisible powers because we easily understand that it is for our benefit, happiness, and well-being to obey their respective laws. It is the exact same situation with GOD/JESUS (except we seem to rebel against HIS laws). The only difference with GOD/JESUS' laws is that oftentimes there is a delayed reaction in the consequences to breaking HIS laws. Like when you see bad people enjoying wealth and fame or simply getting away with crime after crime. GOD/JESUS wants to give us every opportunity to repent and turn away from the bad things, but HE will not wait forever (not that HE bestows punishment, HE just simply and eventually turns away from you). Hence the delayed repercussions of bad people, bad mistakes, or bad decisions we have all made. GOD/JESUS (I say it again) is no one's bitch; therefore, HIS laws will be enforced in the ultimate end. Now then, this is not to take away from the grace JESUS gives because none of us are able to abide by GOD/JESUS' laws 24/7. What my angle/point is, is that GOD/JESUS' laws are there for our benefit not because HE's trying to be a Dictator. After all HE is constantly working miracles all around us in order to spare us from our own mistakes. Do you know what a miracle really and truly actually is? A true miracle is when GOD/JESUS temporarily removes the repercussions of a universal law having been broken. Like when a mother easily lifts an entire car off of her trapped child underneath. Or a man cut completely in two pieces not only lives but grows back ten plus feet of intestines, which the doctors had just removed trying to save his life (see the TLC/History channel documentary *The Day I Almost Died:* episode "*The Bruce Van Natta story*"). That is what a true miracle is, when GOD/JESUS intervenes between HIS natural set universal laws to save us. The Bruce Van Natta story is the ONLY person in the entire series in which The History channel could not prove his healing was anything except a "true miracle" and, of course, Bruce is a Christian. The entire point of the series was to prove miracles don't happen and GOD is *not* real. Bruce's miracle ended up proving just the opposite.

Now let's talk about more natural laws of the earth and the universe—for instance, gravity. The invisible laws of gravity are such that if you jump off of a bridge, you will fall to the earth, which will stop the fall. You may not survive, nonetheless, the earth will stop the fall. Gravity cannot change its invisible laws because someone doesn't abide by or believe in them. Even if breaking the laws of gravity will result in death. It is all up to us to understand and learn how to work with all of these invisible laws and powers. Again, here we see more "freewill" choices. That's why that old saying is as follows: "we will need a miracle to save us," because the only ONE that can save you after having broken an invisible universal law is THE ONE whom created the invisible universal laws in the first place, GOD/JESUS! A miracle is the only time where GOD/JESUS will not change the invisible laws but disrupts them momentarily.

Gravity is an invisible GOD/JESUS-made natural law, which was set into place at the beginning of time for mankind's benefit (exactly like ALL the other laws/rules HE's put into place). It is our responsibility to learn how to use gravity to our benefit, just as we must with all invisible universal laws, even GOD/JESUS' laws, the Ten Commandments. Gravity's invisible laws cannot be changed. Gravity was created for our benefit, to keep our feet on the ground unlike in outer space. Gravity can be and is very beneficial;

however, it can also be extremely dangerous if we do not follow its invisible laws. Like everything else, there are rules and laws to be obeyed in order to enjoy the benefits (for our own good). Yes, even GOD/JESUS' laws, when followed, are ultimately, ONLY extremely beneficial to us.

Keeping all the aforementioned in mind for comparison, let's think about the Ten Commandments which are GOD/JESUS' laws (to protect us from ourselves only for our over-all, ultimate benefit) for mankind. They are exactly like the invisible laws of gravity; for example, they are to prevent us from harm and to benefit us all at the same time. GOD/JESUS is not some kill-joy dude out to spoil everyone's good times.

Look at it like this: Do you get mad at gravity when someone gets drunk and starts dancing around the edge of a forty-story balcony then falls to their death? Well, do you get mad at gravity? No, that would be illogical, most just get mad at GOD/JESUS even though HE told us (in The Bible, man-kind's instruction manual) not to get excessively drunk and stoned. You never even consider getting mad at gravity because it would be absurd to get angry with gravity, right? You can clearly understand it's not gravity's fault someone got stoned, lost control of themselves, and fell to their death.

This example brings to mind one of my favorite Bible verses in Proverbs 19:3 (MSG) "People ruin their lives by their own stupidity, so why does GOD always get blamed"? INDEED, INDEED, INDEED!

(Note: There are many versions of The Bible. The version I have quoted here is The MESSAGE Bible version (MSG), which is like The Bible in everyday street talk as you can plainly see by the way that verse reads. The MESSAGE Bible is my favorite go-to and is my suggestion for your first journey reading through a Bible.)

When GOD/JESUS said things like "don't have sex with anyone you are not married to" a.k.a. the Seventh Commandment "Thou shalt not commit adultery" (KJV)—(adultery being: to have sex with anyone you are not married to). GOD/JESUS is trying to protect us from ourselves and all the massive problems that come along with doing that. What I mean is how many fights and murders could have been avoided throughout history by following this one rule? Do you realize how many people are in jail today because they had sex with someone they were not married to, then a pregnancy developed which caused said person in jail to commit murder or some other horrible crime. Or just simply not paying child support at all (even that will land you in jail). Feeling trapped by a pregnancy causing someone to panic and do things in reaction to that stress. Or maybe it was the continual child support payments which lead to some unmentionable crime or simply flat-out jealousy. There are millions in jail around the world for that one thing (the repercussions of having sex outside of marriage), just watch any number of those documentary-type murder/crime channels. Actually, if you watch those murder/crime story channels, you will see a lot of broken Ten Commandments leading to death, prison, and pure endless misery.

Let's take another one of GOD/JESUS' laws: "keep the Sabbath Holy" a.k.a. the Fourth Commandment—"on that day no one . . . may do work" (NLT), this means take a day off and remember to thank GOD/JESUS for sending HIS Wi-Fi. Again, GOD/JESUS is trying to protect us from ourselves.

Do you realize how many people have run their bodies into the ground working 24/7? These people typically end up stuck in hospitals and, in general, suffering through life with a body unable to function properly (I should know, because I was one of them for the past twenty years). How do you think I learned these wisdoms; it was through much sinning, pain, and suffering.

Actually, the entire law book of GOD/JESUS (The Bible) talks about ways to prevent our bodies from breaking down. Example: don't eat pork (Leviticus 11:7), don't eat shellfish, and don't eat fish without scales (Leviticus 11:10-12), why? Because pork is full of fat, cholesterol and massive bacteria which the pig has no way of digesting or filtering properly due to the way its stomach processes food. Shellfish are basically bottom feeders, they eat the garbage on the bottom, and they are also full of the bad cholesterols, fats, literal garbage, and bacteria. Fish without scales, many times, are also bottom feeders and again they live off the trash (feces) of all other fish, ducks, turtles, etc. Come to think of it, all the above named are garbage eating creatures. GOD/JESUS is not saying that you can't go to heaven if you eat those things, HE is, however, telling us that if we *do* eat those things, then our life on Earth will be filled with sickness. HE is simply trying to guide you on how to best take care of your body, like an instruction manual tells you the best ways to keep a product working to its best potential.

It's a wonder our population is as big as it is with so many of us eating so much literal garbage. Don't think that I have not eaten those things, I was a catfish and pork addict growing up in the South and I've had all the health crises to prove it.

All of the above just goes to show GOD/JESUS is really going to incredible lengths to help us live even when we are doing everything we can to poison ourselves with the food we eat.

To sum it all up, GOD/JESUS has created the entire universe, Earth included, with invisible laws and rules set in stone, like the laws of gravity. HE did this for our benefit so that we would always know some things for certain, like fire will burn you every single time. Do you get mad at the fire when it burns you? No you don't get mad at the fire because it is illogical. Why then do we get mad at GOD/JESUS when we do not listen to HIM or read the instruction book on how to safely live life? Why? I am not saying things will be absolutely wonderful and perfect in life if we follow GOD/JESUS' laws (that's because of satan). However, we can have a much, much easier way if we will only do as HE has directed (for our own well-being).

For all the aforementioned reasons and many more, that's the situation we find ourselves in. GOD/JESUS does not change—EVER—and it is for our own good that HE doesn't. This way we always know where we stand with HIM. We know without a doubt that HIS invisible laws are solid like aerodynamics, gravity, etc. So just follow them already, the same as you do the invisible laws of the universe! After GOD/JESUS set up the universe with all these invisible laws, then HE sent an instruction book to go with everything which is The Bible, the human beings' instruction book, mankind's owner manual.

GOD/JESUS wrote The Bible by using man in the same way we use a pencil to write things down, so man was

GOD/JESUS' pencil (this analogy I heard from street evangelist Ray Comfort) in writing The Bible. If you will look in The Bible, you will see the answers and warnings to all of life.

Would you purchase a top of the line, very expensive product you are unfamiliar with and then throw the instruction book away before you even use it once? Well, going through life without a Bible is the equivalent of doing just that.

Understand, GOD/JESUS has sent us an instruction book on how to live a pretty good life. This book comes with all the basics of every instruction manual out there: troubleshooting, warnings, directions, etc., HE wrote this book (using man as HIS pencil) in the form of different true stories, situations and parables of The Bible in order to make it easy for us to comprehend (*The HelpFinder Bible: NLT*, has those type of subject titles so that you can look up what to do in certain situations).

GOD/JESUS is also streaming HIS Wi-Fi 24/7 for extra help, which is THE HOLY SPIRIT. That is what GOD/JESUS' Wi-Fi is and THE HOLY SPIRIT is ever present, just waiting for us to talk/pray!

Last, but certainly not least, GOD sent HIS only SON down here to help us. HE knew many of us would refuse to read HIS Bible or connect to HIS Wi-Fi, and do you know what we did to HIM (JESUS)? We tortured, abused, and murdered HIM—slaughtered HIM worse than an animal. Mankind did that, not any certain people or group, but mankind as a whole. And if mankind had the chance today, we would probably still kill HIM because we struggle tremendously to understand such a greater intelligence, kindness, and unconditional love/forgiveness. What more do you want from GOD/JESUS? I heard an awesome comparison from Pastor Doug Batchelor on Trinity Broadcasting Network. He said, "There was a father and son out in the ocean for a boat ride, the son had jumped in the water to swim when the father (still in the boat) saw several sharks swimming rapidly towards his son. Thinking quickly, the father cut his wrist with a razor and jumped in the water, swimming the opposite direction of his child. The sharks, of course turned away from the child and went after the bleeding man. When the boy looked at his dad, all he saw was churning, bloody water." Now the question is, if that boy does not take that opportunity to swim to the boat and get out of the water, is there anything more that the father could do to save his child? And so, like that child's father, JESUS came down here and bled, drawing satan and his crew (the sharks) towards HIMSELF so that we could escape. If we do not take advantage of the FATHER'S sacrifice, then what more can HE do? Seriously?

GOD/JESUS (our FATHER/SAVIOR) is PURE LOVE and love never forces anything on anyone; "free will" is how GOD/JESUS exist.

Evil, however, does force things upon us—like a criminal, satan will steal, hack, and take advantage anyway he can. The devil is the ultimate hacker and rapist of souls. GOD/JESUS, on the other hand, will never force us to connect with HIM. GOD/JESUS wants to be loved freely (just like us), without having to force someone to love HIM, so GOD/JESUS leaves it up to us to choose.

"BIBLE":
Basic
Instructions

Before
Leaving
Earth
(I'd heard Pastor Greg Laurie say that on Trinity Broadcasting Network.)

Here's something that will blow your mind, the majority of our laws in the United States of America actually came from The Bible, mostly with in the chapters titled "Leviticus" and "Deuteronomy"—so go look it all up, it's so amazing. For example:

Deuteronomy 15:1 (MSG)
"At the end of every seventh year, cancel all debts."

This law is within America's financial laws to this day for certain debts.

Deuteronomy 17:15 (NASB)
"You shall in fact appoint a king over you whom the LORD your GOD chooses. One from among your countrymen you shall appoint as king over yourselves; you may not put a foreigner over yourselves, anyone who is not your countryman."

This is another law that stands in America today, you must have been born in America to run for President of the United States. Actually, this Biblical law from GOD/JESUS is the law within many other countries around the world, stating that you must be born in said country in order to run for leader/president. We can find GOD/JESUS' laws from The Bible throughout the entire world. This should not be shocking because The Bible has much influence over many countries. America's foundation, however, has more Biblical laws still in effect than most because the entire reason America was even formed in the first place is so that people who wanted to live surrounded by GOD/JESUS, HIS WORD and HIS Law —The Bible—could do so freely.

Last but not least, if you are interested in the influence The Bible had on the laws of America, then you absolutely must look up Justice Joseph Story's writings on the subject. Justice Joseph Story (1779–1845) known as the primary founder and guiding spirit of Harvard Law School, as well as, sat on the Supreme Court. Justice Story based Harvard Law School on strong Christian beliefs, though it is no longer that way today, nonetheless—Harvard Law School began as a Christian Law School. Justice Story also wrote many of our United States laws of today via The Bible's direction, which you may read about in his many, many writings on American law. Justice Joseph Story's writings & biography are still mandatory reading for many law school/Universities to this very day. There is a huge statue of Justice Story in front of the entrance to Harvard Law to this day.

For more information on Justice Joseph Story and Biblical American laws and Christian history of America, please refer to books and video by Mr. David Barton political activist & American historian. Mr. William J. Federer, writer and Christian historian. Also please see the book *GODs Influence in the Making of America* by Donald S. Conkey published by BookLogix.

CHAPTER 3

WAITING IN LINE TO SEE GOD

Here I will try to explain the reason why GOD/JESUS absolutely must remain invisible, just in case you have ever wondered. Ponder this food for thought. What if you could have a face-to-face, sit-down meeting with GOD/JESUS? What would that type of access do to the world? What would that do to "free will"? Let's say that you could get in line to talk to GOD/JESUS any time you had a problem. Right off the bat, the entire world would pretty much stop. Everyone would be in line waiting to talk to GOD/JESUS to complain, to ask for money, to ask what to do every hour of every day. No one would ever even try to do anything or figure things out for themselves. "Free will" would not even exist at all. No one would ever be able to feel that sense of accomplishment because all people would do is get in line to see GOD/JESUS again and again and again.

Would a baby ever learn to walk if we never put it down? GOD/JESUS had to put us down (on Earth) in order for us to learn things and to grow. If access to GOD/JESUS was given in the form of a face-to-face meeting, then all people would ever do is get in line to see GOD/JESUS with their problem of the hour, get it solved, go home, find another problem soon after and be right back to get in line again.

"Free will" would be nonexistent there by demolishing our chance to love GOD/JESUS and freely choose HIM unconditionally or not.

That waiting line would be the sum total of existence. Waiting in line, who wants to live like that? One (not all) of the most important reasons we are on Earth, is to learn and mature and grow and of course, to choose GOD/JESUS or not. That's the whole point of even being here and living life. If all we did is wait in line for a GOD whom we can visibly see then nothing would ever be created by mankind. Yes, GOD/JESUS could supply everything from TV to technology to automobiles to airplanes. If GOD/JESUS did just give us all these things it would leave us humans as mindless blobs of flesh and bone. We would have no sense of accomplishment. We would not be able to grow mentally or spiritually enough to make a clear and conscious choose, which is the entire point of our separation from GOD/JESUS. We are not on this earth to sit around in the lap of luxury enjoying only pleasurable experiences. We have technically left home (heaven) to attain an education here on earth by solving problems and enduring some pain & suffering. This education we are here to gain will be hard work (if we want to graduate back to heaven) just like attending college, where some will take it seriously and others will stay stoned, partying the time away.

Compare physical access to GOD/JESUS 24/7 (to answer

your every request), to a heroin addict with an endless supply of heroin. Said person will simply lay there in the same place as long as they are given the drug and some food and water. They will simply lay in their own filth doing the bare minimum because they have no reason to get up and do anything.

This is what would happen to mankind if GOD/JESUS was physically accessible and visible. We would never do anything for ourselves, ever! We certainly would not—could not—grow and learn because we must experience problem-solving with some pain & suffering in order to learn and grow. If we had full access to GOD/JESUS we would just lay around or be standing in line 24/7.

All that defeats the entire purpose for us being down here on Earth in the first place. The best way I can explain it is like this:

Have you ever dealt with someone, say a small child (which is what we are to GOD/JESUS), even when you absolutely know, without a doubt, what they will do in certain situations? You try to tell them, "I know what you will do," but they fight with you, insisting that they will not do such and such. They tell you repeatedly that they won't do what you're expecting them to do. Yet in the end of said situation, sure enough, they end up doing exactly what you (as the adult) knew they would do. The very thing they *swore* they would not do. GOD/JESUS trying to reason with us would be like you trying to reason with a four-year-old child! It's impossible without said child's growth, education, life experience and yes, even some pain & suffering (which is the only way to really grow, learn & mature).

In summary, that's the situation with mankind and GOD/JESUS. That's why we need to come to Earth and have the human experience. So that we can become educated and have the chance to choose, the opportunity to decide for ourselves, where we will spend eternity. That is "free will"!

Yes, GOD/JESUS does already know what we will do, however, *we* do not know what we will do! Of course, we all think we know, but until we are actually in a particular situation we really cannot say.

In reality, we are proving to ourselves the reasons we will or will not spend eternity with GOD/JESUS in heaven. "Free will!"

The aforementioned are only a few of the most basic reasons we are on Earth. Imagine your hanging out in heaven and GOD/JESUS comes up to you one day and says, "you're out of here, you are going to spend eternity in hell." That would make no sense to you because you have no knowledge of what you did wrong, even though obviously GOD/JESUS has full knowledge of something terrible that you have done.

GOD/JESUS could tell you what you are going to do or not do, but GOD/JESUS is fair, HE does not change; therefore, HE must allow us to show ourselves the reasons for where we end up. Hence life and "free will" on earth.

We all hate it when someone predicts us doing something unwise. However, would you rather have the "freewill" opportunity to make a mistake or would you rather just be told you were going to make that mistake, then automatically be sent to permanent prison (hell)? Life is the trial, the court room is Earth, JESUS is our attorney, and GOD is the judge.

If we are given the opportunity to choose, then we can learn and grow and prove to ourselves what we will, in fact, do.

If there is no "free will" then I guess we just sit in a corner of heaven being told we would screw things up if we tried to do anything. Who wants that? Not us and certainly not GOD/JESUS. Would it not hurt you to see your child locked in a corner? Well it hurt GOD/JESUS to see us locked in heaven with no knowledge of free love's choice and "freewill" choice. Remember that saying, "if you love something, set it free, if it comes back to you then it is yours, but if it doesn't, it was never meant to be." That saying was on posters all over America when I was growing up and of course, I had one as well with a beautiful horse galloping away. I would think about it all the time and ponder its deep meaning. GOD/JESUS loves us, so HE had to let us go in order that we may choose HIM unconditionally (and HE us). Or in other words, the ones that come back to GOD/JESUS will not cause war in heaven (the way satan and his crew did) because they are truly in love with GOD/JESUS. GOD/JESUS' goal in everything is to attain a lasting peace and eternal love in heaven (our family home) for all time and beyond. This, in turn, is why we must all (each one of us eternal beings) come to Earth, grow and learn, then make our choice, because there must be peace in heaven. If we chose well then all the pain & suffering endured on Earth will be erased upon our arrival to Heaven for eternity.

Let me ask you this, who wants to live with someone that you have to force to be with you? Without life on Earth and "free will," that's what the situation would be in heaven with GOD/JESUS. Who wants to live with someone that has not chosen freely to be with you, to love you? Who wants to be in a relationship where you are doing everything, giving everything, and you know the person you love is always doubting being with you because they've never known anything else? No one wants to be used, not even GOD/JESUS. We all want unconditional, true love and GOD/JESUS is no different—after all, we were created in HIS image. GOD/JESUS is the epitome of love, HE *created* love, so it stands to reason that any kind of questionable love for HIM, will hurt HIM.

No one wants a person to pretend to love them only for what they can give them (for instance, eternity in heaven/paradise). This is how GOD/JESUS feels and why HE has given us "free will." Without a downside then how can we comprehend true love to differentiate between good and bad? Earth is the downside and heaven is the upside?

As far as judgements for our "freewill" choices here on Earth, and who actually puts us in hell, were one to go to hell.

The best way to explain this scenario is as follows: Have you ever done something you are definitely not proud of? Have you ever done that something and then turned around only to find out that someone saw you do it? Well, you know that felling of terrible shame that comes washing over you like a waterfall the moment you realized someone you respect saw you? I guess you could say that you are internally placing judgement on yourself, right? Your own feelings of shame and embarrassment are condemning you within yourself. Listen, I do not know everything there is to know about GOD/JESUS and heaven and hell and The Bible, however, from what I have gathered, there is a book of life and everything—I mean *everything* we did in our life on Earth is in that book. When we die, we must then go before

GOD/JESUS and a review of our life is played back with just you and GOD/JESUS watching everything you ever did, which was all recorded in the book of life. As certain things play through, you will have different feelings, like when you did something good and kind, you will feel proud of yourself and very happy that GOD/JESUS is there to watch it with you. Then say one of those terrible moments starts to play, on Earth you were alone when you did the bad thing, but now you are standing right beside GOD/JESUS as your bad choice plays out, that feeling of shame and embarrassment you will surely feel, that waterfall of horror that rushes over you, that you are standing right beside a FATHER who is pure love: That feeling right there, that is the thing that will send you to heaven or hell. In summary, really you are the one judging yourself! GOD/JESUS, being pure love, HE will not send you to hell, it is really you who judges the you within, the emotions you have and feel, as your book of life review plays.

At the ending of your life review, whatever the feeling is within your soul, happy or disgusted, that is what dictates you going to heaven or hell. Here's my two cents worth, it does not matter as much how you start out in life. What is of extreme importance is how you finish, because how you finish is what will give you that feeling of happiness or disgust at the end of your life review/judgement, and it's just you and GOD/JESUS standing there. If you did not accept GOD/JESUS' sacrifice of dying on the cross for our sins, then at the end of your life review there will be GOD/JESUS bleeding and hanging on the cross with your sin all over HIM. That is what GOD/JESUS and you both will see at the end of your life review. It will hit you all at once that GOD/JESUS' suffering before you, is in-fact, your fault. That disgusted feeling will rush over you, and you will fall to your knees. Looking up at GOD/JESUS with tears coming out of HIS eyes, while you fade away to a permanent, solitary prison in hell for eternity. If, however, you did choose to accept GOD/JESUS' sacrifice of taking our sins on HIM, then at the end of your book of life review/judgement, you and GOD will see JESUS come walking up in full white attire (the resurrected JESUS). Then GOD/JESUS will be gleaming with joy because HE knows you choose HIS love all on your own with completely "free will"!

Hopefully you will have chosen GOD/JESUS' great sacrifice for all your sins before you come to the finish of your life review, because if you did not then your very own emotions will condemn you to hell and there is absolutely nothing GOD/JESUS can do about it to save you. "Free will," please remember it!

The last thing I will say about this is that eternity is forever! In the big picture of eternity, it can be compared to all the grains of sand in the entire ocean, that will only be the beginning of eternity. Now take one small grain of sand out of all those grains of sand, that's your life span on Earth, one grain of sand represents your lifetime on Earth! The rest of all those grains of sand, that's just the beginning of eternity. That's how long a person would be suffering in hell, burning. Stuck for eternity with the one and only entity (satan) that hates you more than anything else in the entire universe.

CHAPTER 4

JESUS: WORLD RENOWNED ATTORNEY/DEFENDER

Now I'm going to try and explain how JESUS is the password and transmitter for GOD's Wi-Fi/THE HOLY SPIRIT. First, let me go back to an earlier comparison, gravity. The "LAWs" of gravity are the very essence of gravity, it is what gravity actually is! Without the laws (of gravity) then gravity itself would not—could not—exist. As with gravity, the laws of GOD/JESUS are also the very essence of the universe and the heavens and all existence, the glue which holds it all together. The laws of the universe must be upheld or the very universe would begin to fall apart, one domino at a time. For this reason is why someone had to pay for our crimes and sins, or it would break GOD/JESUS' universe/internet. May I repeat:

The "LAWs" of Gravity are the very essence of gravity, it is what gravity actually is! Without the laws of gravity, then gravity itself would not—could not—exist. As with gravity, the laws of GOD/JESUS are also the very essence of the universe, the heavens and all existence, the glue which holds it all together. The laws of the universe must be upheld or the very universe would begin to fall apart, one domino at a time. For this reason is why someone had to pay for our crimes and sin, or it would break GOD/JESUS' universe/internet.

Therefore, all laws MUST be kept in check, including payment for crimes, sins, and breaking the universal laws, GOD/JESUS' laws a.k.a. The Ten Commandments.

As GOD/JESUS always does, HE provides an option for us, a way of escape.

This is why GOD/JESUS died on the cross and not each one of us, individually. GOD/LOVE provided this emergency exit, JESUS THE CHRIST! Because someone as pure as JESUS died for all of our crimes, sins, and breaking of universal laws. That act alone put the entire universe back in order for the rest of eternity.

Please see Joseph Prince's Calvary Animation Video "What Happened At The Cross" via the internet (four minutes). It will show you in video what I have just described.

Now I will tell a very popular, mainstream parable to try and explain it even further.

Let's say you were arrested for killing someone while driving drunk, now you are looking at a massive problem. You have a court hearing to determine what your punishment will be. Keep the understanding that because you did something against the law (remember "the laws" chapter) that you must now endure some sort of punishment/reaction for your having broken the law (just like you would endure a reaction if you broke the laws of gravity). Knowing the situation you are in, the next step is to hire yourself an attorney to defend you. You will, of course, want the very best attorney since the entire rest of your life hangs in the balance, your future and where you will be living out the rest of your years on Earth.

The going rate for a top-of-the-line attorney to represent someone for vehicular manslaughter/homicide starts at around $50,000 (for the best). Just to get started, that's just the deposit, which means, of course, you will have to come up with several thousand more (if you want the best) by the time it's all over. Even then there is no guarantee you will escape serious prison time.

Now say the very best attorney in all the world heard about you needing someone to represent you and save your very life, and this awesome attorney decided to come to your aide and defend you. So, the attorney shows up to meet with you to discuss your case, etc.

However, you have a problem because you don't have any money to pay this great attorney, now what do you do? Your talking prison (hell) or freedom (heaven), so what else can you do except admit your problem (no money and your guilty) and confess all you have done to get yourself in this entire situation, then ask for forgiveness and help. The world-renowned attorney, known for compassion and great acts of kindness, says he will in fact represent and defend you pro-bono (absolutely free of charge). Well, right then you have a tremendous amount of relief, until you start thinking about the judge and his job to carry out justice "by the book"! The judge cannot be swayed, he must rule by the law, if he does not, then he would not be in the position he is in, as an honorable judge who upholds the law (remember the chapter on laws and miracles). Laws do not change just because we wish them to—

remember the laws of gravity—when they are broken the universe reacts even if death is the end result. If a law is broken someone must be the recipient of the universal reaction (or the dominos would start to fall through-out the universe).

So, your trial day is now here, and you go before the judge then your awesome, kind, compassionate, forgiving (your debt) attorney gets up before the judge and says, "Hello, Father, this is John/Jane Doe, and I am representing them. I'm asking that you allow me to take their punishment." The judge (Father to your attorney) says that he will accept his son as a substitute in place of you receiving the universal reaction to having broken a law. Now your punishment falls upon your attorney, and you are free!

After your attorney has endured your punishment, what would you do for that attorney? Common sense says you would befriend Him for the rest of your life. If He ever asked you to do a favor for Him, would you? Remember, this attorney will only ask you to do good things to help Him with others in the same situation you were in and/or to simply try to stay out of trouble (sin), to show Him that you were worth the suffering He endured for your freedom.

The analogies are in the characters of the story: you are you, the world-renowned attorney is CHRIST JESUS, and the judge is GOD THE FATHER. The punishment for all mankind was JESUS hanging on that damn cross! Why so harsh a punishment? Because the punishment must fit the crime! The crime is all the laws of GOD being broken by all of humanity. Which then caused JESUS to endure one massive punishment (by HIS own choice) rolled out on to HIM at one time from the beating to the cross!

The prison option is the analogy to eternity in hell. The attorney taking your place and setting you free, that freedom is the analogy to heaven. So, let's review:

Prison = Hell
Freedom = Heaven
Your ATTORNEY/DEFENDER = CHRIST JESUS
THE JUDGE/THE FATHER = GOD
The court room = Earth

Again, here we go back to "free will." You must choose JESUS as your DEFENDER/ATTORNEY if you want freedom on Earth and after death in eternity. CHRIST JESUS is THE JUDGE's/THE FATHER's/GOD's only SON, perfectly pure. There are no other (pure, having never sinned, never broken laws) choices out there as far as a Universal DEFENDER, REDEEMER, and SAVIOR. For all of the above reasoning, is why accepting JESUS is the ONLY way to heaven and eternal freedom. Only a PURE (never having sinned) BEING/ENTITY /SPIRIT can volunteer to step in and take our punishment, that's what erases your sin—the PURITY of the PERSON taking the punishment. In other words, the PURITY of CHRIST JESUS' life on Earth is what erases a lifetime of sin. Please see the film *The Chronicles Of Narnia: The Lion, the Witch, and the Wardrobe* (2005 written by former atheist C.S. Lewis); The Lion is GOD/JESUS when HE is slain in the film, it will give you a great understanding of what I am trying to explain here. Back to my explanation, if you would rather take the reaction/punishment to each of your own sins as you do them, then you would end up suffering around the clock because our sins (breaking universal laws) are daily and, as law breakers, all we can do is pay for each broken law at a time. The power is in the "PURITY" of CHRIST JESUS, because of HIS perfection, HE can swallow the entirety of all humanity's sins (law breaking). Like when someone is falsely arrested and put in prison for years of suffering. There innocence (purity within the falsely accused situation) causes restitution to be paid (in the millions of dollars) to said person the moment they are proven innocent. That's the type of innocence I am speaking of except on a much, much grander scale—an eternal scale. The worse the punishment of the innocent person, the more restitution is given. CHRIST JESUS suffered the longest, slowest slaughter and torture of any innocent human who has ever lived on the face of this Earth (see Mel Gibson's *The Passion of the Christ* from 2004). The Bible tells us that HE was beaten and tortured so badly that HE was unrecognizable as even a human at all! Due to the severity of HIS punishment (as an innocent man) CHRIST JESUS was given restitution in a massive amount by the universal laws order to keep things in balance. CHRIST JESUS then took that restitution and gave it all—in its massive entirety all of it, if it were in dollar form, trillions and trillions and trillions—JESUS gave all of it back to HIS CREATOR and FATHER in exchange for all of us, anyone who is willing to accept CHRIST JESUS restitution. GOD/JESUS gave everything owed to HIM for false arrest and turned it all over to us law breaking sinners if we will only accept HIM/JESUS. Like a person with (false arrest) millions who is trying to share it with you, then it is up to you to make arrangements to pick it up a.k.a. accept.

GOD/JESUS will forgive us for anything and everything with the exception of not accepting CHRIST JESUS' suffering on the cross. In other words, not accepting JESUS as your ATTORNEY or HIS false-arrest millions is the one and only unpardonable and unforgivable sin in the entire universe.

Did you know the entire world keeps time according to CHRIST JESUS existence? Well, it's true. The year 2022 is a counting of the years that have passed since JESUS was on this Earth in human form.

I would like to close this chapter with one more description of THE SACRIFICE of all time for us:

Colossians 1: 15-20 (The Message Bible)
> **15-18.** *"We look at this SON and see the GOD who cannot be seen. We look at this SON and see GOD's original purpose in everything created. For everything, absolutely everything, above & below, **VISIBLE & INVISIBLE**, rank after rank after rank of angels – everything got started in HIM and finds its purpose in HIM. HE was there before any of it came into existence and holds it all together right up to this moment. And when it comes to the Church, HE organizes & holds it altogether, like a head does a body.*
>
> **18-20.** *HE was supreme in the beginning and – leading the resurrection parade – HE is supreme in the end. From beginning to end HE's there, towering far above everything, everyone. So spacious is HE, so expansive, that everything of GOD finds its proper place in HIM without crowding. Not only that, but all the broken & dislocated pieces of the universe –*

people & things, animals & atoms – get properly fixed and fit together in vibrant harmonies, all because of HIS death, HIS BLOOD that poured down from the cross."

CHAPTER 5

Gold Is Purified by Fire, Man Is Purified by Gold

Pastor Andrew Womack said, "there are more people destroyed by wealth than by poverty." Truer words have never been spoken. Just look at the life of John David McAfee (1945–2021). Genius computer programmer, he is a prime example of wealth having destroyed a man. How sorry I am for the loss of this man's potential. When you wonder why GOD/JESUS will not give you endless money & influence after every prayer, please remember HE maybe trying to protect you from a catastrophic life such as Mr. McAfee's.

Gold must be melted down in order to burn all the impurities out. Once liquified through intense heat/fire, gold will separate from all the other minerals, impurities, etc. Then you can easily remove the junk which causes the gold to be impure. Likewise, a diamond is created by enduring thousands of pounds of intense pressure over hundreds of years. The pearl is created when a small grain of sand becomes trapped inside of an oyster. The oyster then becomes very uncomfortable and extremely irritated, at which point it begins to spin the grain of sand around to try and create a buffer around the irritating grain of sand. It starts coating the grain of sand with a shell-like material in order to make it smoother, softer, and less irritating. From all that uncomfortable irritation, the beautiful pearl is created.

If you think about it, the more pressure, fire, heat, and extremely uncomfortable irritation anything endures, the more it is worth and the stronger it becomes! This is how all the precious materials of the world are created, even us humans. Anything worth having (even a good and happy life) must endure all or some of the aforementioned unpleasantries. Such is life. Have you ever seen a home that was burned down to the ground, where the only thing still standing was the fireplace and chimney? Why does the chimney survive the fire (of an entirely brick-built home) and not crumble to the ground like the rest of the bricks of the house, why is the chimney the only thing (brick) still standing? Because it had endured years of small fires which prepared it for the big fire. That's me, I've been through many a small fire so when the big one came, I was conditioned for it, I knew how to handle it better than some (I'll get into my story later). For that reason, I am still standing.

Now put mankind under all those same unpleasant circumstances.

As I mentioned in the title of this chapter, man is tested by gold. GOD/JESUS is ever watchful, and HE sees deep into our hearts, how we act when we gain wealth. Gold/wealth puts man in the fire and under pressure, so that as fire burns out all impurities from gold, then [the striving for] gold is man's fire which brings out all the good, bad, and the ugly of his/her soul. It will go one way or the other, there will be those who recognize GOD/JESUS has given the wealth (should we attain it), and those who refuse to recognize GOD/JESUS at all. When we endure pressure, heat, and extremely uncomfortable irritation for long periods of time, that is how GOD/JESUS develops us, we gain wisdom, we become more and more developed like the diamond or gold. Like how weights and exercise force muscle tissue to become stronger, so it is with problems, stress, crisis, and of course wealth (gold). Not only do we develop strength but wisdom and worth, as well. Let's look at exercise in detail, like how exercise and weightlifting forces muscle development. Suffering forces spiritual growth to form the best us we can be. Likewise, we become sore and experience pain as we exercise, but "no pain, no gain" isn't that what is said about physical fitness? In exercise and weightlifting, we readily accept pain and suffering because we understand the benefits outweigh the suffering.

In the same way, suffering through trials and tribulations actually benefits us because we learn things which will greatly benefit us in the future.

When we exercise or lift weights, we are literally tearing up our muscle tissue. You are destroying muscle tissue which in turn causes the regrowth of much stronger muscle tissue. This is how our muscles become stronger. We begin to look better and feel great, pretty soon we have forgotten the pain and suffering it took to get fit. We know that there will be yet more pain and suffering to come if we want to maintain our toned bodies, yet we are not scared of that suffering to come.

We are not freaking out at the very thought of going to the gym, because the pain and suffering that come with exercise, is to be expected. Suffering isn't fair or nice, even when suffering is beneficial, yet why is beneficial suffering accepted in some situations and not accepted in others (like when GOD/JESUS doesn't seem to be listening)? This is where faith comes into play, we must endure suffering with faith because faith will determine what benefits the pain and suffering endured will give us. If we go through suffering without faith in GOD/JESUS, then it was worthless, and the devil will reap and hack the rewards of all you went through. So, if you want satan the hacker to reap all your rewards just lose (or don't have any) faith when enduring some terrible situation! When I have been in one of my hundreds of serious sufferings and wanted to hate GOD/JESUS and give up my faith, I would always imagine satan laughing out loud because he accomplished his agenda of proving to GOD/JESUS I did not really love HIM enough to remain faithful during all of my trials (which were considerable even if you live in a third world country). When I would picture satan laughing at me, something inside me would remember all GOD/JESUS' words from The Bible, Christian TV, and Christian music. Then I would know for a fact that things would get better eventually if I did not lose faith. If you do not read The Bible or listen to Christian music or TV then you will have nothing to pull on, no hope, you won't even have the strength to tell yourself with assurance that this too shall pass with 1,000 percent certainty! What I do know, as a Christian and from years on end of serious pain and suffering, is that all sufferings for Christians are only temporary, but all sufferings for the spiritually unprotected is guaranteed to be endless and worthless (of no gain). I have lived on both sides and yes, my pain only increased daily while satan rode my back, he had hacked into every part of my life. Upon my escape from him by running to GOD/JESUS (even with my huge bag of sin), I felt an almost immediate release of much of my pain (physical & mental). I am speaking from much horrific experience for years and years on end (which again, I will discuss later).

There are so many people since time began that have endured a crossroads, decisive moment like mine and much worse.

Throughout the history of the world some of the wisest leaders have been those who had endured great sufferings while establishing their faith in GOD/JESUS, then attaining leadership positions—Abraham Lincoln is one of many that comes to mind, he struggled with the existence of GOD/JESUS in his younger life then right before he was killed, he and his wife had planned a trip to Israel to see where JESUS had lived. Many of us know some of the most successful people who had hard childhoods. Many of the successful people of today grew up in poverty, working for hours on their family's farm every morning before they even went to school, and then came home and worked until late at night as well. The lessons they learned in all that hard work, pain, and suffering day in and day out caused them to understand how to achieve success in their adult lives if they were smart. Both my father and my stepfather were men like that. Heads up, do not be like me, late to the realization that an invisible GOD/JESUS is in fact the only way in which HE can really exist.

If you will simply be still and think, then you will see that the entire world is, in fact, GOD/JESUS' chalk board. HE's using Earth like a teacher uses a chalk board to show us how to live and achieve the best out of our time on Earth.

Look at the mother and baby eagles as an example. Before mother eagle will even choose her "lifetime" mate to have babies, she will test every male eagle who comes to her. She will go and find huge, heavy limbs broken off from trees, then fly up very high and drop the limb. This is to see if the interested male eagle will be strong enough to catch the limb and return it to the female. If he can catch the heavy limb and return it to her several times, then she knows that he will be strong enough to do the same when they are teaching their babies how to fly. Once mother eagle has her "lifetime" mate, then she can begin construction of the nest. When the mom first makes her nest, she puts the pointy sticks, thorny shrubs and hard materials in the very bottom of the nest, then she places a layer of smooth leaves for cushioning. Next, she places rabbit fur, rodent furs, and other very soft materials which the baby eagles will sit on when they're born. As the babies grow older, the mother eagle knows her babies will not willingly leave the nest for any reason, not even for a short walk. Keep in mind mother and father eagle are still having to feed these huge babies and clean all their poop, etc. Mother knows what she must do, so she starts removing the fur parts of the nest. Every day she removes a little more of the comfy stuff until the pointy sticks and thorns are making the babies more and more uncomfortable (GOD/JESUS does this same thing to us in order to get us up and moving). Finally, they leave the nest. Did you see how mother eagle caused her babies more and more discomfort until it became unbearable, at which point they finally start learning to walk & soon fly. GOD/JESUS does the same with us, making us uncomfortable in order to force us to grow. Now mother and father eagle must teach them how to fly. Here's how the flying lessons go, one of the parents will push one of the babies off the edge (they nest at the very top of mountains or the tip tops of the very tallest of trees). The parents then fly beside their falling baby as it struggles (scared to death) flapping its little wings, then right before it hits the ground, father eagle will swoop under the falling baby and catch it on his back. He then takes it back up to the top of the mountain or tree nest and they push the baby off again and fly with it again until it almost hits the ground. Again, father eagle swoops under it, picks it up, and repeats this until the baby learns how to fly.

This is how GOD/JESUS teaches with us! You think your falling and under great pressure, it feels like you have a fire under you, which pushes us to accomplish our goals and dreams. The next thing you know, you're soaring above it all just like an eagle because GOD/JESUS has come to swoop you up at the last moment! That is "IF" you're with GOD/JESUS and are connected with GOD/JESUS' Wi-Fi/THE HOLY SPIRIT. If you are not, then all of your suffering will have been in vain. Let's face it, life is hard, and suffering cannot be avoided; however, we can minimize our suffering and use the suffering that we must endure, if we choose to access GOD/JESUS' Wi-Fi.

The Bible (humanity's instruction manual) is full of stories like the baby eagles. Not so much with animals, but true stories and parables of men and women in all the necessary situations we need to know about. Stories of each and every situation we could ever face while on earth. These stories show us what not to do, and also what GOD/JESUS expects and wants us to do for our own best interest. GOD/JESUS will only ask and guide you to do things that will benefit you in a healthy way first and foremost, and of course, what benefits you (in the long run) makes GOD/JESUS so very, very happy.

Now look at the other side, if you choose to do life without GOD/JESUS' Wi-Fi. Then the one pushing you over the edge will be satan the hacker, and you can seriously forget about him swooping under you at the last moment to save you. The devil will even try to bait you or tempt you by showing you a better way, an "easier" way to learn how to fly, easier than, say, trusting GOD/JESUS to swoop in and pick you up at the last moment. The hacker satan will make you think to take the easy way, but history proves time and time again "no pain, no gain"! One thing I've learned about GOD/JESUS' personality from reading and rereading The Bible in all of the most popular different versions and through my own sufferings, HE waits till the very last minute to swoop in and help, nonetheless, HE always shows up just like the rising sun! Many say GOD/JESUS does this so that we know for a fact that it had to be GOD/JESUS, so we as Christians don't think it was all our doing. GOD/JESUS lets us come to the end of our own efforts, then HE shows up to let us know two things: HE loves us a billion, trillion times more than we love our own children (and ourselves), and that HE wants us to have and experience true freedom to choose, "free will."

Another one of GOD/JESUS' examples, is in the very food we eat. This has to do with that age old saying "you will reap what you sow." The word "reap" means to receive back what you put out (multiplied), and to "sow" means what you put out into the world. This is not a bad thing because it goes that when you "sow" good this means good will come back to you multiplied, and whatever you "sow" will always come back in much larger numbers than what you originally sowed. Just remember it works when you "sow" bad as well, bad will return to you multiplied! GOD/JESUS shows us perfect examples of returns a.k.a. "reapings" in the food we grow. We plant two little kernels of corn and from that comes a huge corn stalk, which produces several hundred more kernels of corn. It's the same with most all the food we grow in the world. Again, I say, the world is GOD/JESUS' chalkboard, and HE is the teacher. GOD/JESUS put this lesson right in our face, I mean we eat every day, so the lesson is up in our face all the time—literally in your face. Now understand, this is one of those universal laws so if you do "sow" something good, it will eventually come back to you multiplied allowing you to "reap" what you "sowed." However, keep in mind if you do something bad, then that will also come boomeranging right back to you in spades as well. If you decide to cheat someone, thinking you will gain something, just remember, you may well gain what you want in the present time, however you—yourself—will be cheated somewhere in the future at least double if not seven to a hundred-fold in the same way.

CHAPTER 6

FINISH YOUR GAME

Here is the best way I can describe the entire situation of what we are doing here on Earth and why we are here. The situation is this, there was heaven way, way, back in the beginning. Then satan became bloated with his own beauty and wanted to take over heaven and put GOD/JESUS below him. The devil went around heaven talking to anyone who would listen, recruiting every angel he could to be on his side—to vote satan in and GOD/JESUS out. Next, there was controversy and unrest in heaven so GOD/JESUS threw satan and his crew out of heaven. There's GOD/JESUS in heaven with unrest. GOD/JESUS said, "There will never be unrest in heaven again!" When satan started his campaign to take over heaven, GOD/JESUS then knew that before any beings could be allowed to stay in heaven again, that each one would have to be given "free will" to decide a head of time before they were permitted to just automatically be allowed to stay in heaven. After all, satan was created and just allowed right on into heaven which gave the devil no choice or "free will," he simply did not understand how good he had it because there was nothing to compare goodness with before satan went rogue. The devil actually created evil within himself by challenging GOD/JESUS a.k.a. LOVE, hence the reason for his rebellion. GOD/JESUS said, "never again," and HE meant it!

We all start out with GOD/JESUS, then we must come to Earth where we can exercise our "free will" to decide for ourselves where we want to spend eternity, heaven or hell. It's all up to us.

When we come to Earth, when we are born, a veil is placed over our memories of GOD/JESUS. This is done because there must be a fair playing field. GOD/JESUS must see our true feelings for HIM. Will we love HIM for HIM, by faith alone without remembering or knowing the full scope of all HIS true beauty? We must be able to decide to go to GOD/JESUS without any knowledge of what we can gain if we do so. GOD/JESUS doesn't want groupies, HE wants true, unconditional love just like we all do.

GOD/JESUS wants to know that we will choose HIM unconditionally. It's kind of like somebody who really loves you and ask you to marry them. As far as you know, they earn a good lower or middle class living, you agree to marry them then after the wedding you find out you have married a multimillionaire! There are many people who do just that, right here on Earth, to make sure they are really loved. Of course, GOD/JESUS already knows us inside out. However, in order to keep confusion out of heaven, HE must allow us to experience our own choice. This is so that we can show ourselves what we chose, then we will always have that memory of "freewill" choice no matter where we end up, heaven or hell, we will then understand we are the ones who chose where we ended up for eternity.

If we could remember heaven and GOD/JESUS, there would be no "freewill" choice to be made. Of course, we would choose to go to GOD/JESUS if we had memories of HIM because the beauty would overwhelm us, then we wouldn't even stop to consider actually loving HIM for HIMSELF and by faith alone.

Look at it like this, coming to Earth is like going off to college to become wise and make decisions. We are down here to choose and to learn to choose, then and only then, can there be peace in heaven for eternity.

There is a movie called *Jumanji* (1995) I am speaking of the very first movie only. It's a great example of what happens if we choose GOD/JESUS. So, remember how the kids go through all kinds of challenges throughout the entire film? They even grow-up and older while they are experiencing their ordeal. Look at the end, where the game ends and everything goes back to normal. Even though things all return back and corrected, even though the people grew up while they were playing the game, they return back to being children after they finish the game. There is one huge difference, they kept their memories and knowledge gained from the game's experiences. So much so, that when the two older children grew up, they remembered that the two smaller children's parents were going to be killed in a car accident, so they were able to prevent their deaths. In the end, the knowledge they retained from the game/experience was of great benefit far into the future with lasting and eternal effects! That's a good example of what our life on Earth is like.

You MUST finish your game/life (just like in *Jumanji 1995*) if you want things to be set right again, and to finish the game is to achieve true faith in GOD/JESUS (and HIS sacrifice) before you die, because if you do not, then the game will simply continue even after death—except that your suffering will be a million times worse than anything you experienced on earth. Nothing can be set right. So please finish your game, do your own research on GOD/JESUS. See the movies:

> *The Case for CHRIST* (2017), based on the book with the same name, written by Lee Strobel (former atheist). This man was bound and determined to prove there is no GOD/JESUS and so he studied and traveled, speaking with scholar's, researching, etc. for years trying to prove his point, only to have GOD/JESUS reveal HIMSELF through out Mr. Strobel's journey time and time again! Lee Strobel is now a Christian teacher, speaker and evangelist today. This film is the true story of his journey.

> *The Chronicles of Narnia: The Lion, the Witch and the Wardrobe* (2005), based on the book with the same name written by C.S. Lewis (former atheist). This film is about GOD/JESUS and THE HOLY GHOST but in a parable form. Previously mentioned but worth mentioning again.

For those of us who choose GOD/JESUS' sacrifice and accept JESUS' representation, we will be like *Jumanji 1995*. All the horror we experienced while on Earth will simply be wiped away. We will return back to our youthful selves and everything we suffered will be completely reversed and made right. We will enter heaven with our loved ones, but still will retain the memory that we experienced "free will" to be with GOD/JESUS. All pain will be gone because everything will be made right. The devil, satan the hacker, will have all GOD/JESUS' wrath bestowed upon him repeatedly throughout eternity for every little thing he had done to hurt us.

Life is like when you go on a business trip. You travel far from home to solve problems, gain knowledge, accomplish goals and make decisions. When you are finished with all the problem solving, gaining of knowledge, etc. what do you do? You get to go home and rest. That's what we will do when we are finished here on Earth, we will be going home to an eternity somewhere, it's up to you where!

CHAPTER 7

YOUR REAL ENEMY, THERE'S ONLY ONE!

> *"For we are not fighting against flesh-and-blood enemies, but against evil rulers and authorities of the unseen [invisible] world, against mighty powers in this dark world, and against evil spirits in the heavenly [invisible] places."*
>
> —Ephesians 6:12 (NLT)

As you may have already surmised, the devil is not your friend. But now let's really get into the situation and uncover just how deep it all goes. Let me propose to you just how badass satan can be. There is nothing, nothing, he will not do in order to obtain your soul only to dump you in a solitude of burning sulfur for eternity (remember eternity's description, all the sand in the ocean still would not cover eternity) upon your death.

There will be no partying or good times with your old buddies if you end up in hell. Everyone is separated, with the exception of hearing screams of tremendous suffering repeated over and over. You will be in complete solitude except for the intervals of demons stopping by to torcher you physically and verbally. (See Pat Robertson's DVD *"Life Beyond the Grave" C.B.N. production,* for legitimate recollections of hell's atmosphere.)

You already understand that the devil can hack into your receiver/soul any time he wants to, if you are not protected by GOD/JESUS' Wi-Fi. Have you ever watched a puppet show, like puppets with strings attached? Well, that's what we are to satan, that's exactly how he sees us human beings, like puppets on strings which he can pull any way he wants in order to do his bidding. The devil is in the spiritual/invisible realm but unlike us, he can see all of our invisible puppet strings. Our puppet strings are any number of things which can set us off. We all have strings, that's what people mean when they say, "so and so sure pulled their strings or pushed my button".

The very best way satan can harm us is by using us against one another, that way we are much less likely to see satan's hand in the situation. When someone really hurts you, maybe in your job, or in financial ways, or in your very heart—you can bet it is satan. He is the driving force behind all controversy, arguments, and hurt feelings since the beginning of time, having started with Eve to harm Adam. The devil wins twice because he not only hurts you, but now he has harmed the other person he had used to get under your skin. When you get hurt by someone, and that hatred is boiling over inside of you, just remember your being played on a grand scale. The master manipulator of the universe (satan) is your real enemy! Not the person who you think is harming you (the person your blaming is being played too, by satan)! You may think you are smart, and in fact your IQ might be through the roof, nonetheless, you are not even close to the intelligence of satan. You have only been on this Earth a very short time (remember, one grain of sand, that's the span of a human life), the devil has been around, sharpening his skills, since the very beginning of time!

Look at this because this is what we are dealing with:

2 Corinthians 2:11 (NASB)
"So that no advantage would be taken of us by satan, for we are not ignorant of his schemes."

(NLT)
"So that satan will not out smart us."

(CSB)
"So that we may not be taken advantage of by satan. For we are not ignorant of his schemes."

1 Peter 5:8 (NIV)
"Be alert and of sober mind. Your enemy the devil prowls around like a roaring lion looking for someone to devour."

(ESV)
"Be sober-minded; be watchful. Your adversary the devil prowls around like a roaring lion, seeking someone to devour."

Job 2:2 (MSG)
> *"GOD asked satan, what have you been up to?" Satan answered GOD, "oh, going here and there, checking things out."*

Listen, whenever you get hurt, don't look at the person who perpetrated the action, you need to look at satan, not people. The devil is the one who causes all people to hurt other people and that is the bottom line. If you are not protected with GOD/JESUS' Wi-Fi, alert and sober, then you can easily be played by satan. We are all in a domino effect type situation, one gets hurt and then due to their hurt, they turn and pass their hurt on to the next person, and the next, and the next, until it gets to you. I must give credit where credit is due, satan is a professional, I mean he really has his procedure perfected. What's that old saying, "hurt people, hurt people," but satan is behind the very first hurt person who started it all.

The devil walked up and pushed one little domino (person), then he reclines back in his chair and has a grand, old time watching us all fight among ourselves. The worst thing of the entire situation is that we allow it to happen without fighting satan back whatsoever. How do we fight back? By attaining GOD/JESUS' Wi-Fi.

We believe in and use everything in the universe, which is invisible, I mean we believe in all those invisible powers like Wi-Fi, satellite, cellular and radio signals, the Cloud, gravity, aerodynamics, the wind, and oxygen (which is so powerful that it rules the lives of the entire Earth)!

We believe in all of the above invisible powers so much that we wrap our entire lives around all of it, I mean we can't even roll out of bed without a cell phone alarm. Yet somehow, we cannot, for our very souls, believe in GOD/JESUS and satan surrounding us in the exact same kind of invisible realm, why?

Personally, I cannot stand anyone to take complete control of my life and mandate every move I will make, day-to-day. Most people feel the same way, we all cherish our freedom. Yet, if you are not receiving GOD/JESUS' Wi-Fi (THE HOLY SPIRIT), then you, my friend, are being controlled and mandated to, on some level of your life, by satan the hacker, just like a puppet on a string. The first step to true freedom is to realize you are being played by satan. Know it or not, if you are not consciously connected to GOD/JESUS' Wi-Fi, then you are being hacked by satan and his minions on some level. Once the devil hacks into your spiritual receiver, he then slowly downloads a virus which reveals itself in the form of thoughts and urges to do things that you know to be wrong. These types of viruses will cause you to question your own integrity.

I am telling you all of this information because I found out the hard way, through much blood, sweat, and many, many tears. I'm not just preaching here and telling you something about all the aforementioned, without any experience on the main subject of satan's torture and suffering bestowed upon mankind. I have tangoed with satan far too long, and suffered more than most, unless you live in a third world country—and even then, it's questionable.

Admittedly, the majority of all my adult suffering was due to my own stupidity and not realizing satan was playing me. Not realizing there is an invisible realm with many dangers. Also in choosing bad men, bad friends, and a bad lifestyle but, most of all, because of not reading my Bible and searching out GOD/JESUS earlier in that invisible realm. Unwilling to listen to the wisdom of GOD/JESUS' instruction manual for humanity, I mean, I don't think I made one correct decision until after thirty years of age, except for having my daughter.

Unfortunately, my daughter was dragged down the same road of pain and suffering right along with me. I am not going to write my entire biography in this section, but I will lay out a summary.

I want to tell you this so that you understand how I came to write this book and also to let you know that I can sincerely understand the pain & suffering people endure. Pain and suffering are the real teachers in so much of life. What I mean is we just do not remember things in life the same way we remember something extremely painful. When something slams us, we not only will embed it into our permanent memory, but the after thoughts of the entire painful situation will continue to teach us long after the event has passed. GOD/JESUS, however, uses our pain (though HE did not cause it) to teach us, which is what HE means when HE said, "We know that GOD causes everything to work together for the good of those who love GOD" (Romans 8:28 NLT). Or "Don't you see, you planned evil against me but GOD used those same plans for my good" (Genesis 50:20 MSG)

At any rate, let's start with before I was even born—my mother (who looked like a mix between a young Elizabeth Taylor & Linda Carter in the '70s *Wonder Woman* series) actually emptied an entirely loaded hand gun at my father while she was nine months pregnant. She unloaded a .38 at him while he was attempting to sneak out at midnight to see his girlfriend/secretary. He survived, and due to his employment

My mother

within local Government, no one went to jail. They both have become practicing, faithful Christians since those days. Next, when I was four months old, I had a massive hernia that almost killed me, which I still have a long scar from to this day.

When I was nine months old, my teenage babysitter got a butcher knife, cut and stabbed up the entire living room, ripping curtains, cutting up the sofas and chairs, stabbing the walls and tables and lamps, all this with me alone in the house with her. We lived in a pretty nice neighborhood and this girl was a neighbor from a very nice and well-to-do family. Nonetheless, having a nice home did not stop satan from attacking my entire family, including any visitors. We had some serious demons living in that house, and they attacked anyone who crossed our threshold.

My father created bugging devices and electronics for law enforcement, and anything else they needed having to do with electronics, he was an electronics genius. Due to his work, he would be given men (who were serving time in prison) as helpers for his electronics projects, all the prisoners loved him because he treated them all fairly and as equals.

During my younger childhood years, one of those men who had worked with my father escaped from prison (he was serving time for murder). Where do you think he came to hide out? You got it, at my house. We were swarmed by law enforcement of all kinds.

Then a few years later, I was about five or six years old, my mother came to put me in bed, and close my curtains for the night (I'd always been terrified of the darkness outside my bedroom windows). When mom started to pull the first curtain closed, a man jumped up in her face. This guy was dressed in dark, hanging, witch-type clothing, multicolored streaks of dark colors, dark reds, blacks, purples, greens, blues. I actually saw him when my mom screamed. He was wearing a large, pointed witch's hat with the floppy rim, and had all those same, dark colors smeared all over his face and hands. You could clearly tell that this was a huge man. My mother started screaming, and we ran to get my father, who went for his elephant rifle and out to chase that (in his words) "son-of-a-bitch" down! Mom called all of my father's FBI, sheriff, and police friends; pretty soon there were law enforcement of every kind with their dogs and a helicopter all descending upon my house, again. Throughout the night, I listened to dogs barking and gunfire and law enforcement everywhere. My father had shot down into the woods while running after the man, but he was gone. When the sun came up, the police found some bloody, ripped parts of the man's costume hanging on a tree branch, but it was as though he had disappeared into thin air. It was so strange, that was my first recollection of being face to face with satan. He never was found, but something strange started happening about two years after that incident, in the form of a stalker. I—me, as a small child—I had a stalker. My father seemed to think this stalker was that witch-man from my window. This man would call when I was home (I had loved answering the phone as a child), so I would answer and he would tell me that he liked what I wore to school that day or how beautiful I was, or tell me when my birthday was, and other creepy things like he was in love with me and would marry me one day. That went on for a while until my father's friends found out who it was, and I never heard about it anymore.

When I was seven or eight years old, late one night I heard a knock at the back door. My parents were asleep, so I hesitated to answer, but I heard a woman's voice begging for help, so I opened the door, and she fell into the doorway with blood all over her head and body. She was almost dead, she had stab wounds all in her head. I was screaming, and my father came running, he told me to go to my room and stay. He called an ambulance and stayed with her at the back door until they got there. I do not know what happened, I was never told.

Soon after that, I was given a kitten and was in our back yard playing with it when a huge wild bobcat (native to the Southern state I lived in) appeared from nowhere, ran up trying to bite my kitten. When I grabbed for the kitten the bobcat grabbed my small hand with its paws and then pulled my hand deep into its mouth, it bit completely through my entire hand! It took forever to fight it off, I was a small child weighing about 60 pds. which was the same weight as the Bobcat. Afterward I was strapped to a medical board and given the old fashion style of Rabies shots, talk about a living hell, satan's been trying to kill me pretty much since I was born. I almost lost my hand from the massive infection that followed which would have been my writing hand.

When I was around ten years old, my brother and I were given an Ouija board for Christmas of all things, by my parents who had no clue what they were doing. The only reason they got it was because that was one of the most popular items sold for that particular Christmas. Soon after playing with it, my father became so enraged one night (after drinking alcohol excessively) that he grabbed one of his elephant rifles and put it to my mother's chest (his eyes were no longer the light blue I knew, but a solid black). I ran in front of the rifle's nose, between it and my mother's chest so it was right in my face and told him, "If you kill my mother you will have to kill me too." For which he replied, "get ready to die!" I kept saying, "No Daddy, I love you" over and over, till finally I could see my father again when I looked into his eyes, the blue had suddenly come back.

By the time I was twelve, I was in my first rehab for drinking heavily and smoking a small zip lock bag of marijuana every day.

When I was sixteen years old, I married my high school boyfriend who proceeded to snort cocaine around the clock and beat me 24/7. I became pregnant and was forcibly taken (by my family members) to an abortion clinic and strapped down to have an abortion against my will. A few days after that, this man whom was constantly beating me, came into the convenience store where I was working. He said he was sorry for beating me and placed his hand, spread flat-out, on the counter, then with the other hand pulled out a huge, long screwdriver and plunged it into the middle of his hand. It went all the way through his hand and deep into the countertop. He said that's what he felt that he deserved for everything he had done to me. My parents had the marriage annulled. When it was finally all over, my father had him arrested and put in jail, where he was beaten just like he had done to me (I only found out about him being beaten years later).

By the time I was seventeen years old, I meet the man who would be the father to my only living child to this day. We were married and then I started to slowly find out who I had married. Prior to coming to the United States, my now ex-husband had been the horse trainer for Pablo Escobar – (infamous Colombian Drug Lord and World leader of cocaine distribution 1949-1993).

My, now ex-husband, was from Colombia, South America, and had immigrated to America. We had a beautiful daughter together, non-the-less, he began to run wild with other women for years on end. I mean his infidelity was almost a monthly occurrence. He was a world-renowned, international Spanish horse trainer, and so had all the groupie girls that entailed. My decision to finally end the marriage came one night when he had attempted to take me to one of those "sex clubs" or "swinger's club.s" He had told me we were going out to a new night club (in one of the four largest cities in America). I had no idea where we were going and so like any other time that we were going out, I got dressed to the 9's. I wore beautiful Colombian emeralds & diamonds accompanied by a Halston dress and Manolo Blahnik heels. Let me say that we were not even in the same state we lived in and I didn't know anyone in that city. At any rate, we finally arrived at the night club. Upon entering the front door there was a lady with towels and bags telling me to remove all my clothing and put the towel around me (the bag was to put my clothes in). I looked at my husband and he was already taking off his clothes. I started crying and ran out to the car and just stood in the dark parking lot for at least ten minutes. Finally, my husband came out telling me that I MUST go back in with him and take my clothes off because he could not enter without a woman with him and they would not let anyone enter with clothes on. When I absolutely refused, he then put me in the car and drove to one of the most infamous & dangerous locations in that state. The next thing I knew he was putting me out in the middle of the road at 12 a.m. on a Saturday night. I watched him drive away, down the road he stopped to pick up a prostitute (I'm guessing so he could go back to that club). I was just standing out in the middle of hell, scared to death, complete with my high heels, Halston dress and several pieces of flashy "real" jewelry. I was crying when out of nowhere this sweet elderly angelic black lady came driving up to me and said, "get in right now"! I asked her who she was and she said GOD/JESUS had sent her to pick me up. I got in with her and as she drove me to a hotel, she told me that she had been to an all-night Christian Revival close to that bad area. They had been praying all night for the crime & murders there to stop. She got me to the hotel and prayed with me at the door still sitting in her car. I got out and turned around to look back at her once more and ask for her contact information but she was gone! Completely gone! She must have been an angel because there is no other explanation!

I do want to say that the way my husband treated me that night was not normal for him. Yes, he had cheated on me through-out our ten years together behind my back, but he was never abusive or put my life in danger ever before. He had been drinking and snorting cocaine all that night, which again was NOT something he frequently did. So there again I saw first-hand how a demon can hack into your very soul through too much drink (spirits) & drug. Because the man who dumped me out at midnight was NOT the same man I had been with for years.

After that experience and all the years of his infidelity, I decided to get a divorce. I had to beg him to file for the divorce because he never allowed me access to any money. Through-out the next year he repeatedly tried to force me into visiting sex clubs. Looking back, I now realize that he had an extreme "sex-addiction" & desperately needed help. Finally, after a year of begging, he filed for divorce. He told me, point blank, that I would regret it till the day I died, and he was right! He said he was going to take away the one thing I loved more than anything on the face of this earth, my daughter! He said he wanted me to feel the pain I was causing him to feel by taking away the one thing he loved, which was me. I didn't believe him, but I soon would. Shortly after, we were involved in almost ten long, hard, tortuous years of a child custody battle. Every time I would gain custody, he would actually make things up to lie about and accuse me of something else to go to court over. Pretty soon I was out of money and out of health from all the stress and threats.

Throughout my daughter's childhood she would call me crying saying someone had beaten her or molested her, etc. This would set me off to go try to rescue her. I repeatedly went through this, several times every year, for close to ten years, traveling from across the entire country many times (due to work) to try to help her. Several times I ended up in jail for attacking the person who had harmed my child, or for confronting my ex-husband's drug-addicted girlfriend for beating my daughter for any number of reasons. Anything could set her off, mostly that I was the child's mother. Let me tell you, when you have money like my ex-husband had access to, you can pretty much do anything you want with just a slap on the wrist. He became a real professional at using the United States court system to continually torch me. I do want to make something crystal clear about my ex-husband (my daughter's father), he personally never harmed our daughter himself, that I know of. He had to travel constantly for his work, so he was never home. Therein lies the problem, he was so desperate to dispense his punishment on me (my punishment being to never see my child again), he would leave her with anyone—willing even to break the law to keep her away from any contact with me, be it in-person or over the phone. So, it was never my daughter's father who would harm her, that I know of, but the different people he would leave her with—they were the culprits. Through the years, after I had gotten Child Protective Services involved repeatedly due to my daughter's complaints, I would beg him to just let me care for her. That I would not date or go out anywhere ever. I told him that I did not care how many women he brought home, but just please let me care for our daughter at our large horse ranch's guest quarters. This offer really made him angry, it insulted him that I did not care how many women he dated. It made him even more angry that I loved our daughter enough to be willing to sacrifice my life to be with her and raise her. Even if I had to live in complete solitude. He wanted to know why I didn't love him like I did our child? So, back to custody court we would go for years.

The entire situation is so very sad, because my ex-husband had been a kind man when we were younger. He was the first person to teach me that if you passed by a homeless person that you should go get them something to eat and drink. He would say, "never give them money but always give them food and water." We actually toke Arthur Blessitt (2009 "The Cross" Documentary) some food & drinks as he passed through our town while carrying that huge cross around the entire World. My ex had grown up in the backwoods of Colombia and had seen severe poverty all his life. He had many good qualities, but like one of those top-of-the-line computers that can be hacked into (though he believed in GOD/JESUS, he did not check his Wi-Fi connection every day, hardly ever, and neither did I) satan the hacker, deceived my now ex-husband, and took him away from us, time after time. We had the American dream, and we both let satan-the-hacker, destroy it all.

Now here I was with no formal education or income. I had agreed to let my ex-husband have everything in the divorce, all the property & money, everything. I didn't even ask for alimony because, frankly, I knew that would be my death sentence. All I wanted was my life and my daughter. Horses had been the only form of income I had ever known up to this point in my life. I had left school at 17 yrs. to start traveling & working horses with my now ex-husband. My extensive knowledge on horse management, breeding management, embryo transfer, shipping eggs & semen on nitrogen, etc., however, did not help because my ex-husband was known around the world. No one would give me work within the horse industry per his request. I needed money to continue the court battles to try and protect my daughter. I had stumbled on to one of Oliver Stone's film sets. Having heard they needed a horse rider and they were paying $500–$1,000 per day. That was just what I needed to pay for more courts and attorney fees for my daughter. At that point my employment choices to make the amount of money I needed (for constant year-round Attorneys) were slim to none. Especially since I had no education.

Oliver Stone ended up getting me into the Screen Actors Guild Union. Due to the good Union money, I would travel all over the country working on Union film sets with my Union card. Amazing, the irony of the very man who actually wrote the script for *Scarface (1983)* is the same man who would, years later, give me a hand up towards fighting for my daughter.

I was able to travel because every time I would get custody, my ex would swiftly file suit again & again with several high-powered attorneys. Filing for emergency temporary custody using false accusations as usual. If he could not attain his daughter immediately through those tactics, then he would simply hire someone to disappear with her during one of his weekend visits. They would keep my child in undisclosed locations for months. Yes, this is possible in America. I would call police and tell them the aforementioned situation to which they would tell me that I would have to take it up with-in the court systems. This left me without my daughter over and over. So I traveled for Union work living out of my car for most of the custody battle (which was years and years). I was required to maintain a home in the county where the custody court was located if I were to have any chance at regaining my daughter. So then I could not afford two separate homes, this is why I ended up living in my car repeatedly. Most of the Screen Actors Guild Union work (for the good Union money) was either in New York, Texas or Los Angeles. I remember living in my car keeping a big container of dried instant oats with a bowl so that I could go to gas stations and ask if I could use their microwave to cook it. A couple times I had no food and had become so hungry that I would get dressed in a business suit (to blend in with everyone else) then go to one of the really nice hotels which had self-serve hot breakfast. I would just walk in as if I was staying there and help myself to all I could eat. The few times I had to do that, I did have at least two dollars to place in the tip jar. Luckily, I was never confronted.

Ten years into all that, my body and mental state broke down. This, in turn, caused me to spend more than five years in a back bedroom of my mother's home watching Trinity Broadcasting Network "TBN" (Christian TV) around the clock. After all else failed, I threw myself 1,000 percent into seeking GOD/JESUS. How stupid I had been not to have taken this entire situation to HIM at the very start. Going in and out of the hospital for more than fifteen different major surgeries. As well as a couple of short mental institution visits in between due to having tried to commit suicide several times. Two of those times I was in a coma for a minimum of five days in the hospital, where I should have definitely died (I actually have had three medically documented "Near Death Experiences" through-out my daughter's being abused/kidnapped years). I ended up stuck in bed from a number of serious illnesses and surgeries. During all those years of being in bed and watching TBN-Christian TV around the clock, I see now that GOD/JESUS was using all the bad that happened to turn for the positive by using my bed ridden time to teach me about life and the invisible spiritual realm. Also having read through the top-seven versions of The Bible repeatedly, front to back. Of course, GOD/JESUS is the ONE who has really put it together and called my attention to all the invisible powers around us. I was constantly studying GOD/JESUS around the clock, trying to figure out how to overcome what was still facing my daughter and I.

At any rate, in-between, when the custody battle first began and my health collapsing (which would finally stop me from responding to any further custody court hearings), I repeatedly tried to get remarried. I thought that would solve all my problems because a married person has more of a chance at gaining custody than a single one. Just so you know, there is no person on Earth that can solve your problems. Only a relationship with GOD/JESUS can solve problems & give you true happiness. This is what I found out—as usual—the hard way, through extreme suffering.

Let me sum up those guys: (Please keep in mind, all of these relationships happened during a time span of more than ten years, they did not all happen back-to-back but spread out through the years.)

The first guy was the owner of a prominent airline out of South America. He had been an acquaintance I had known through the years. He was really trying to help me to keep my daughter because he had seen how all of my mutual friends with my ex-husband had taken his side, unconditionally. I was taken out and shown what happens when someone dared to try and help me. I saw about ten men beating and kicking the South American airline owner. He was on the ground, and they were still kicking him, he was bleeding all over his face and head.

Please keep in mind all of my travels were at times that my ex had either taken our daughter and had someone simply disappear with her for extended times, or he had filed more court dates after I had won a custody hearing, and then taken her away until said hearing with threats in between that I would be killed if I continued to bother him via courts or police (I did both anyway, but to no avail). One time right after my ex had told me a specific friend of his was going to kill me himself (verses put a "hit" out on me), I had ended up in the hospital on life support, not expected to live due to unending stress causing my body to start shutting down my liver, kidney's, etc. I had been placed in that section of the hospital where they keep people who aren't expected to live. So there I am for twenty days when I saw my ex-husband walking past my room with the family of the very man who said he would kill me just a month prior. Turned out, less than 72 hours after that man had made that threat to kill me, he dropped dead at his home of a massive heart attack & brain stroke! The ambulance had resuscitated him. Now there he was on the same death-row hospital floor as me. I am not proud to say that he passed away after suffering greatly right down the hall from me. My ex-husband had always been superstitious, and so after that, he never threatened to have me killed again. At least not to my face.

After my life calmed down a bit from the airline man, I then went to Venezuela for a weekend at the request of a gentleman who had been one of the few friends from my past who was still speaking to me. He was deeply involved in Venezuelan politics and was friends with the countries president Rafael Caldera (1916–2009). I was still very ignorant about World politics. After my arrival, I was picked up by his brother, who was surrounded by gunmen. He had done some bad business deals with Colombia (I would later find out). They had, in turn, shot his daughter in the head (she was three years old) while she sat in the back seat of her mother's car at a red light. The brother who had picked me up that day is now dead. Need I say that things simply did not work out in this relationship?

Next was my surgeon fiancé who wanted me to do *Playboy* magazine (again I thought only about money for my daughter's on-going custody battles). My thinking was, at least Playboy was a tasteful magazine which many a gorgeous movie star had posed for. However, prior to a photo shoot I needed a breast lift. I had breastfed my daughter for one year, causing minor breast damage. My surgeon fiancé and one of the top-rated plastic surgeons of the state, gave me a breast lift to prepare for the *Playboy* test shoot. During the surgery they accidentally punctured my lung (then conveniently forgot to tell me). My lung filled with blood and began to rot, until a month later when I passed out. This landing me in the Emergency Room with a near death, septic-shock situation for one month and many surgeries. When I finally left the surgeon, he would send me "666" messages any time I would leave for local TV Union work. I did not know while dating him, but he had a real romance going with the devil and "666," of course, was satan's number. I never did do *Playboy* magazine because of the lung injury, taking more than two years to recover from multiple surgeries. For the record, I have never done any kind of nude magazines or professional porn film work. I say this because one of these men I discuss had released multiple pornographic videos **(which are not me)** to the internet titled with my Screen Actors Guild Union name. It was in an effort to damage my legitimate theatrical and feature film professional Union credits. I am working with an internet investigator to track the source of these videos, in order to prove, in a court of law, the attack on my professional Screen Actors Guild Union name from this individual. This man has placed more than 10,000 video's on youtube alone, with my actress name and has continued this childish attack for more than 15 years now. My goal in this is to sue this individual with the financial benefits going to support rescued child victims of sex trafficking. This is just one more of satan's attacks which I will flip on him. Causing something satan meant for bad to become a benefit towards GOD/JESUS' work in rescuing children.

At any rate, once I finally recovered enough from the lung surgeries to go back to work (part-time locally), I started work at an Italian restaurant as the front hostess. I meet one of the owners who was very familiar with my locally infamous child custody battle of the ages! He understood that I needed money to continue to hire attorneys. He knew if he introduced me to a nice-looking, financially stable, gentleman, that I would probably be inclined to date/marry him in the hopes I could get help in retrieving my child. What I did not know; however, is that upon the introduction to aforementioned described gentleman, I was being sold for $5,000. When that man invited me on a beautiful weekend vacation trip, I readily accepted. I had been under so much stress in recovering from the lung surgeries for the past two years and really needed a rest. This man had been the perfect gentleman, very clean cut, and a retired (higher-up) politician for his state. Once I got there, we got into a small disagreement. He then informed me that he had, in fact, purchased me for the previously stated amount, and that I better start being more cooperative. The guy that had sold me, I found out, had been involved in some very serious missing persons (plural) situations. I stayed with the politician I was sold to for almost six months before all my crying over my daughter drove him insane. He actually hired someone to pack me up and take me back to the same state where my daughter was living. All I can say about that situation is that I was under so much stress from my daughter's calls of serious abuse, along with my depleted half lung situation, that I was not paying attention to my surroundings. I was close to insanity by this time and still in major recovery from the long hospital stay and surgeries due to my rotting lung collapse.

I stayed single, just working on local union commercials and film sets or modeling for car rentals, The Home Shopping Network, local lotterys, luxury hotels, etc… for a few years and being with my daughter, as much as possible. Spending every dime fighting to protect her. I then met a very nice local equine veterinarian, who owned one of the top equine hospitals in the area.

(Again, all of these different situations were spread out over a ten-year period, also this was right before social media and background checks were the norm.)

Finally, I thought, I can settle down. What I did not know, was he had been married to a pediatrician in the opposite end of the state. He had two children with her, which now he was court ordered not to see. Their mother had placed a permanent restraining order on him due to molestation charges of their small children. It all started coming out when I meet his neighbors a few months into the relationship. They were very nice, clean-cut Christians, who took in and cared for foster children. I had walked over one day to just introduce myself. They warned me that this guy had come over one day when the children's dog had gotten out to his property. So he, the vet, dragged the dog over to their house and slammed it down, then gave it some kind of injection, at which point the dog died, right there in front of all the foster children.

I, of course, left and moved immediately, (I had been living with this veterinarian in order to save money to put toward attorney/court cost for my daughter). A friend of mine owned several townhomes within this same county that the vet lived. One of the townhomes was unoccupied and so was offered to me as temporary shelter. These townhomes were part of a private, huge racetrack training facility for racehorses, complete with a stallion barn which housed several million-dollar thoroughbred stallions (plural). This vet guy came over one night, or early morning, and burned that stallion barn to the ground with all the horses still in it! I guess he wanted to thank my friends for giving me a place to stay.

Last but not least, was the criminal defense attorney – one of the top three in his state with "death certification"; I do not even know where to begin. From his sadomasochistic interest (which I had no clue about). To [cheating on me by] having affairs with men, to his law firm partner (who he was about to split a multimillion-dollar case) going missing off his boat, found floating in the ocean, never to be seen again to this day. All of the aforementioned on this man, came out within the last week I was with him. When I had seen the passports of two of the 9/11 terrorist pilots inside of his home wall safe. He said he was trying to sell them on the black market. The two terrorists, in particular, had taken their flight lessons (to fly the terrorist attacks) at the same airport where this attorney (I was dating) had his airplane garaged. I do not know any of the details, he simply had his safe open one day when I walked in his home office and he showed them to me, bragging of what they were. That last week with him was enough for me to completely forget about remarriage as any kind of answer. A few years after having left this man, a young girl was found dead in his home hanging by a noose. He told everyone she had committed suicide. He has since been connected to several other suspicious deaths without repercussion thus far. I have prayed for his soul in the hopes that he may eventually be arrested. If incarcerated he could possibly have a chance at listening to GOD/JESUS' word in prison there by saving his soul as well as stopping him from any further damage. After this breakup, my health finally collapsed and I really started to chase after GOD/JESUS 24/7.

All of the aforementioned are simply the highlights of satan's trail on me. It doesn't even cover any of the day-to-day situations endured.

All that being said, I think I can tell you with experience that satan is definitely very, very, real. The hacker satan, will chew you up, kick your ass, and spit you out in a hundred different directions. The ONLY, ONLY way I have EVER found to protect myself from these massive attacks, is by hooking up with GOD/JESUS' Wi-Fi, THE HOLY GHOST.

When I say that I understand a person's suffering, please believe me, I really do. I remember being on my knees, on the floor, screaming at the top of my lungs, with a loaded gun in my hand, because of another call from my innocent child crying at having been seriously abused yet again, and begging me to rescue her. All the while, knowing there was nothing I could do except go to her, be arrested, and then sit in jail again until my elderly parents pulled more of their savings out to pay my bail. Here was the bottom line with my daughter's situation: I had promised her, if she would just tell Child Protective Services what she told me, I promised her, she would not have to go be hurt ever again. Well, she did tell, and she was with me until a team of attorneys came in and rapidly got visitation reestablished with her father. The next time I saw my child, she said her abusers had beat her up for telling on them. My understanding is that somehow her father had no knowledge of these beatings. This same situation repeated itself again, at which point my daughter stopped telling authority about her abusers for fear of being beat, etc. At this point, she would call me telling ONLY me the latest in abuse. I would go running, but when I would go to officials for help (the same people who had promised to protect my daughter if she would just tell what happened). They would promise again that she would not have to go back to her father's if she would just tell them what happened. She knew if she told again that she would eventually end up back at her father's and someone would beat her up or possibly kill her (which is what she had been told) for telling on them. Again, I say all this was happening with people her father would leave her with, never did her father, himself, harm her, that I know of. This cycle went on and on for many, many years. Her calling me with the latest serious abuse and me calling police, sheriff, etc., only for her to be too frightened to actually tell the authorities what had happened. Even with physical proof, like broken arms and iron burns shaped like a clothing iron on her body—I mean perfect imprints of an iron burned into my baby's skin—they always had some excuse of some accident that caused it. Believe me, I use to beg and pray for death. If not to escape my daughter's incurable cries, then it was to escape all the physical & mental pain I was enduring. It was inescapable for almost ten years, this went on day-in and day-out! I can't count the times I lie on the floor, like that scene from the movie *The Shack* (2017), I would scream "I'm sorry, I'm sorry" to GOD/JESUS while holding a gun to my head, because I could not take the torture any more but I could not leave my daughter behind like that either. Every time I watch that scene, in that film *The Shack*, it all comes rushing back.

Listen please do not be shocked at the horror's my daughter & I endured due to all those years of child custody battle. Those types of custody battles are an absolute epidemic in the United States of America still, to this day! Not only with the torture being bestowed upon the mother in the custody battle but also towards fathers as well. It all depends on who has the most money. The person who has the most money can easily use the American "justice" system to torcher and abuse their ex-partner & children for as long as they wish or until they can no longer afford attorneys to continually file motions! I have thought and thought about this epidemic with-in our justice system to try and figure out how it could be prevented in the future but to no avail. The only thing I could come up with is something like, "people going to custody court must have equal attorney power (by law). Or if it is clearly seen to be evident that one parent is using the court system to torture the other for years on end, then somehow, there must be an intervention due to the children involved. However, I don't think any of those ideas would work due to the infringement of other laws. With my case, it would have been easy to prove "torture by courts" due to the fact of years upon years of endless false accusations towards myself, which NONE were ever proven to be fact EVER!!!

Before I end this chapter I would like to tell you of one last heart breaking loss. It's about the stallion I and my ex-husband had raised and trained up together. I was so in love with this gorgeous animal. This was before I had our daughter, this stallion had been our baby before we had children. We would travel all over the World with this stallion on cargo planes in order to attend competitions. This is the stallion I'd mentioned earlier, the "World Cup stallion in our breed of horse". Traveling with this magnificent animal is how we attained the title "World Cup Stallion". I lived with this animal from a baby on through many years. I would sit next to him in the filthy cargo plane while my ex would fly first class. I would sleep in his stall when he was sick. This stallion and I were so close that when we finally did win "World Cup Champion Stallion", they put me on the front cover of the international horse magazine with the stallion (instead of my ex-husband, his rider). This stallion would turn out to be yet one more casualty of our divorce in a horrific way. Because of the divorce, we had to sell this beautiful stallion and so we sold him for $1.2 million. The new owners were residentsce of Colombia, South America where they took my beloved horse. Before they transported him to Colombia, they purchased a million-dollar life insurance policy on him from an insurance company located here in the United States. They ended up being involved deeply with the Colombian Cartel and were arrested a few months after having moved my stallion to Colombia. Now these two men were in big trouble and needed big money in order to pay for a defense attorney to get them out of a Colombian prison. While in prison they borrowed a massive amount of money from with-in the Cartel, promising to pay them back with my stallion's insurance money the moment they left prison. Things went as planned, they were released from prison and went straight to the stallion's barn and did everything they could to kill my horse in a natural way so that there would be no trace of foul play. The only way to kill a horse by "natural causes" is to run him until he can no longer stand then lock him up in a stall with plenty of cold water and rich food. This causes the stomach basically, to explode, causing the horse severe pain for hours, sometimes days, before they finally die a horrifically painful death.

This is exactly what they did to my beloved stallion. The next day they called the U.S. insurance company to claim their million dollars. The insurance company sent investigators to Colombia. After about six months of investigations, the insurance company told the men to come to the United States to their head quarters in order to receive payment. When the men came to the U.S. to pick up their million-dollar claim, the F.B.I. was waiting to arrest them on American soil for insurance fraud among other crimes.

I was happy about that arrest, however, it did not bring my beautiful stallion back to life. He was only ten years old upon his death. I can still imagine him suffering and suffering just wondering where I was to help him, to rub his belly, to make him feel better. Once again, I had been brought to my knees with a broken heart! I cried so hard that I thought my heart would come up out of my chest. That situation happened about the same time I became bed ridden for those five years. Just so you know, I had already been crying on a daily basis for my daughter. Most nights I would wake up screaming from nightmares of my baby being abused. So when my stallion was murdered I guess it was "the last straw"!

By the time my daughter finally turned eighteen and gained her freedom, I had turned into "the walking dead"!!! I was nothing but a breathing bag of bones begging GOD/JESUS to please just let me die already!!!!!!!!!!!!!!!!!!!!!!!!!

The only reason I have written about my personal experience is so that you will know that I have truly suffered in just about every way humanly possible. I do want to, once again state that I am not saying that I never did anything wrong during all of these situations. Because I did plenty wrong and I mean plenty! Nonetheless, whatever situation you may find yourself in, be it self-inflicted or forced upon you, I am telling you, flat-out, that there is absolutely no way to over come the invisible realms of attack without GOD/JESUS' Wi-Fi!!!

Now going back to the start of this chapter, satan uses us against one another. The devil actually tricks us into hurting each other through selfishness, pride, greed & being offended. These are satan's top four tools to baiting us into harming one another. Don't fall for it. Any time you start feeling anyone of those four triggers then STOP EVERYTHING you are doing and saying IMMEDIATELY!!! Do not react so swiftly because that is exactly what evil wants you to do. Simply wait, do anything you can to stop thinking about the situation. Try not to react until after you've had a full night's sleep. Then when you do reassess the situation remember satan is trying his best to force you to crash & burn right into hell. Whatever decision you make, don't let any of those top four be your guide. I let them all rule my life for many years and you see how that went. Only by the grace of GOD/JESUS have I been able to overcome. The bottom line is that people are not your enemy, satan is!!!!!!!!!!!!!!!!!!!!!

Understand who you are really fighting (satan, not a person), then flip the entire situation on him. Here's an example of what I am talking about. I have stepped back and really looked at what happened to my daughter & I. Next I pin-pointed the very bottom line of where the mentality came from to get such a mind set as the Colombians who supported my ex-husband. Then I found a 100% non-profit Christian organization called "Redeeming Grounds" working in Colombia. What they do is cut down large cocaine fields and then help the farmers replant with coffee beans. In this way the farmers will not starve, they will still have a wonderful crop of produce to sell. After harvesting, the Christian organization "Redeeming Grounds", takes the coffee to market and offers their coffee grounds for sell world-wide. See most of the Colombian farmers growing cocaine really have no other choice in crops to grow unless they want to starve to death. I have been all over Colombia and have seen places worse than any third world country in certain parts. These people have nothing, not even education (which is how my ex-husband ended up at the age of 15 yrs. old working for Pablo Escobar). They have no clue how to sell a legitimate crop on the world market so when those Cartels come along offering to pay them to grow cocaine, they don't have much of a choice between being bullied by the Cartel and being destitute of food, education & even basic medical care. The people that hurt my daughter, myself & murdered my stallion are a direct product of the aforementioned scenario. The beginnings of that entire situation were first put into play by that master manipulator, satan the hacker! Cocaine crops are one of satans vacation homes and so I attacked that!!! Now by promoting "Redeeming Grounds" I am paying satan back something GOOD for his evil towards me. In this way is THE ONLY WAY to really punch satan in the gut! If you will react like this towards all of satans attacks, then satan will discover that every time he attacks you, that you will only do something GOOD in retaliation. Once your reaction is only doing good after every attack, satan will eventually leave you alone because he will know all you will do is good no matter what satan does to you. Now then, if I can turn things around, I know that you can too. But NEVER EVER react in aggressive anger towards anyone because that is exactly what evil wants you to do. Do not play into the devil's will. Do only good, if for no other reason but to piss satan off, until you can get to the point where you can actually see the real benefits of fight evil with only good reactions! Remember, life is only 10% what happens to you but 90% what your reactions are!

"UPDATE: Redeeming Grounds Coffee is no longer active at the moment (though I'm hoping they will one day rise again). In order to continue to promote Christian Colombian organizations, I will thus forward be promoting the following organization which is based in the United States:"

SAMARITAN'S PURSE COLOMBIA, SOUTH AMERICA
P.O. BOX 3000
Boone, North Carolina 28607
(828)262-1980
Samaritanspurse.org

P.S.
I am ever praying for my daughters father, always hoping the very best to develop through CHRIST in his life.

CHAPTER 8

ALWAYS BE ALERT AND OF SOBER MIND
(1 Peter 5:8 – NLT version)

My daughter struggles with seeing me to this day, and I don't blame her. She had been told her entire life, that I just up and left her, that I did not love her. Every time she was beaten or harmed, they would always somehow blame me. Constantly telling her it was all my fault that she was being beaten, etc. At one point, when it seemed I could not get a message to her in any way what-so-ever, I became so desperate to let her know I loved her & was still fighting for her (in the courts) that I wrote about my intense love for my daughter on my IMDb.com film credits & actress page. I knew she would see that. [This was right before any social media was around].

My daughter is the love of my life, after GOD/JESUS, and I pray that we will one day work together for HIM. That she would use all of her pain and suffering to help others recover (with her knowledge of abuse) who have endured similar things as her.

My daughter had a daughter this past January. I said a prayer to GOD/JESUS to please let my grandchild look just like me. I asked this of GOD/JESUS so that every time my daughter looked at her own baby (feeling all that overwhelming love), she would be reminded of my overwhelming love for her and how I still feel about her. I know GOD/JESUS answers pray because my granddaughter looks just like me!

Toward my many faults, most of the things that happened to me as an adult were in fact my fault for not having listened to so many people who GOD/JESUS had sent to me along the way. For as many times as satan attacked me, GOD/JESUS would send someone to counter that attack, and tell me over and over about HIM, GOD/JESUS. Some of what these GOD/JESUS-sent messengers had told me would actually stay with me, like the Angelic elderly black lady. Looking back, those little morsels which stuck with me are probably what acted like seeds, which have now broken through and finally bloomed in the form of this book and my salvation. I also now think that satan knew all along that I would become a street evangelist and write this book. This is why he had been trying to kill me since I was born. Keep in mind that the bigger threat you are to satan's agenda, the more attacks he will bestow upon you. If you are being attacked to the degree I was, then those attacks are positive proof that (if you get with GOD/JESUS like I did) you are sure to overcome it all.

I could have gone either way with what I have endured (even though much of it was my fault for not making better decisions). I could have become so angry and vengeful that I could have destroyed myself. Or I could have indulged in the use of free cocaine and anything else which would numb the pain. However, only by the grace of GOD/JESUS did I grab hold around HIS neck and held on for dear life.

Listen to me, please, the life I had before had been filled with material things. Prior to giving birth to my daughter, I was very materialistic. I thought the world revolved around me, I had new cars, the best horses, beautiful jewelry, and gorgeous clothes, but inside I still was not happy. There was no real happiness in my life up until I had my daughter. After having her, I started looking at all people as someone's baby. This gave me great compassion for everyone. Hence the reason for this book, which is to tell as many as possible of the invisible oppositions we are really dealing with.

I want to make sure I am clear about how much of a wretch I was, how ignorant I was and just how much I have learned about the invisible realms. Let me put it this way, when I was wealthy and had every material thing I wanted, along with an internationally famous Spanish horse-training husband, a beautiful ranch with the World Cup Stallion (in our breed of horse), I was not content and certainly had no peace. These days, I am humbled and giving everything I can to help people, which leaves me close to broke every month. Nonetheless, I am happier now than I had ever been when I was jet-setting around the world on airplanes with our horses in tow, or shopping in Beverly Hills, Miami, South America, etc.

When a ship is sinking (hydrodynamics), going down in a storm, a popular reaction (law of said dynamics) is to start throwing all the cargo overboard. So, the less weight may save the vessel, well that's what I believe happened to me. I was forced (year after year) to throw more and more material possessions away until I had lost everything. Then when you have lost everything material and your health, too, you start to understand that only now (with nothing) your life has actually been saved! Saved from being a wretched, stuck-up, selfish bitch. There is a quote from GOD/JESUS which I never understood until now:

Matthew 10:39 (NLT)
"If you cling to your life, you will lose it; but if you give up your life for ME (JESUS), you will find it."

Take it from someone who knows very well, get rid of material things which are weighing you down. It is much better to just let go of materials (that are nothing compared to your life, loved ones, and your health) than to go down to the grave holding on to them.

This reminds me of yet another lesson from the eagle. GOD/JESUS uses the eagle for many examples throughout The Bible. The eagle loves to catch fresh fish, and so it will swoop down on a huge fish swimming, and like lightning it will lock its talons completely into the fish, lifting it up with its powerful wings, pulling the fish out of the water and on to land.

However, sometimes the eagle will swoop down and lock into a fish which is absolutely too big for the eagle to lift up out of the water. But instead of letting go of the fish, the eagle will refuse to let go, which in turn, causes the eagle to drown itself. People see these majestic birds, just floating downstream, dead—sometimes still locked into the fish they had tried to grab, all because they simply would not let go.

There are many ways of the eagle that parallel with mankind's life, both good and bad. Things we see that can kill the eagle (like not letting go of material things) we should learn from them. (Again, I tell you, the earth is GOD/JESUS' chalk board to teach us). Also, things in which the eagles do to sustain their lives, those we should definitely learn from as well. For instance, an eagle will fly as high as it needs to in order to avoid other birds that are trying to drag them down, steal their food, or just in general, cause them any form of difficulties. An eagle can fly much higher than other birds because of the decreasing oxygen the higher they go. Eagles were made to go above all the rest (hence the reason GOD/JESUS chose eagles to compare humanity with, in The Bible). Their lung capacity can handle extreme altitudes, whereas other birds cannot. GOD/JESUS has made us all capable of flying high, above the riffraff and troublemakers, but we must be connected to HIS Wi-Fi a.k.a. THE HOLY SPIRIT, if we are to achieve great heights. We must attain that invisible power that GOD/JESUS is constantly streaming if we are to indeed reach astounding heights.

Now, I am thoroughly prepared for any attacks satan the hacker will attempt. Once more GOD/JESUS is also prepared to back me up because finally, finally I connected my receiver to GOD/JESUS' Wi-Fi/HOLY SPIRIT!

I heard on TBN one day someone say, "life is 10 percent what happens to you and 90 percent how you react" (I wish I could remember who said this because it's such an intelligent and truthful thought). I still wonder if I had only reacted differently in some way then maybe I could have spared my daughter some or all of her torture & abuse.

Being stuck in bed, in a lonely bedroom, for an entire five years gave me much time to just calm down and think.

A few years into being bed ridden and in and out of hospitals for surgeries to remove several body parts causing potential death, I had become so very lonely and scared. I was still dealing with extremely high levels of stress from my ex-husband's threats and my daughter's cries for help. Finally, my body had had all the stress it could take. I was laying there with terrible chest pain when I got a taste in my mouth, like the taste you would have if you drank a big glass of pure gasoline. This was followed immediately by a pain worse than any lung collapse (doctors say it is the worst of medical pains), which I had experienced earlier with the breast surgery complications. This was much worse pain than a collapsed lung. Within seconds, I was bleeding out with a huge, perforated stomach ulcer. Within the hour, I was being driven at high speed to emergency surgery to try and save my life yet again. The closest hospital that could repair my stomach was an hour away, so the local hospital ER gave me high levels of pain medications and loaded me into another ambulance for transport. The ambulance was running almost one hundred miles per hour with the sirens, and that is the last thing I remembered because I had bled out and died (it was not the first time that I had died).

I woke up three days later in the hospital and I knew what I had to do was work for GOD/JESUS. I felt this very real urging to start studying and listening to all things Christian. That particular "near death experience" took me to a place outside my body, a place of pure LOVE where I know all people belong if they only knew. I became glued to Trinity

Broadcasting Network. I began to tithe to a Jewish-Christian missions organization in Israel because of what I was told while (dead) out of my body, "take care of MY [GOD/JESUS] children & I will take care of your children"! From that day on all I listened to was Christian ONLY. I would not look at anything that could poison my thoughts, no secular news, music, TV, movies or books. All of the aforementioned is what jump started my learning, absorbing, and listening to GOD/JESUS' WORD, around the clock. I found that if I turned off Christian TV at night, it never failed, I would have horrific nightmares. When I would wake up from the nightmares, I would turn Christian music or TV back on and fall back asleep with the most peaceful dreams ever. That is how I learned that you can drive demons from attacking you by playing any form of the Gospel. The hacker satan and his crew absolutely cannot stand to listen to THE WORD being preached or sang about so they will eventually leave. Check out a guy named John Ramirez and his book, *Out of The Devil's Caldron,* or any of his books for that matter. John Ramirez is a former leading satanic priest who is now a Christian. He can tell you all about what satan hates, and how much power practicing & praying Christians actually have over the devil and the world in general. It would blow your mind to know just how much power GOD/JESUS is trying to freely give us in order to make our lives better.

Gallery

My Father

My Mother

Me and My Daughter

Runway Modeling

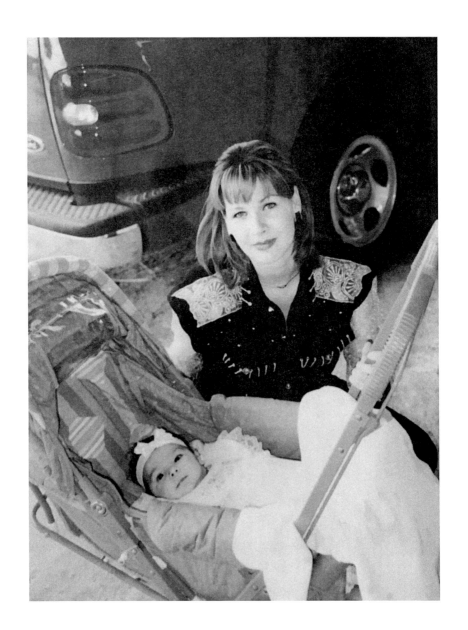

J.C. Story as a blonde

At horse ranch office exhausted & stressed to the limit, near the end of my marriage.

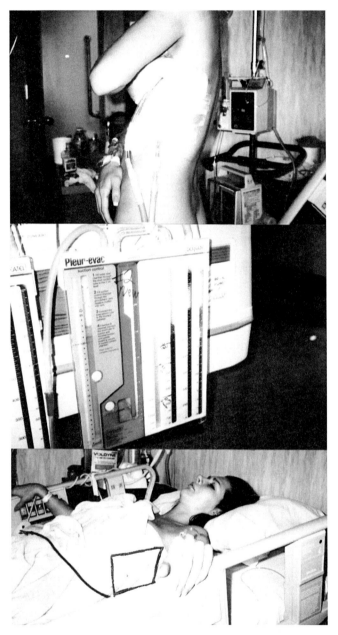

One of many near death experiences. Collapsed and Rotting Lung. (30 days in hospital and 5 surgeries to save me)

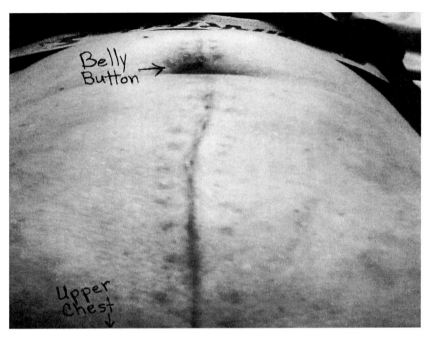

Perforated stomach ulcer where I bled out. Another near death experience. My stomach basically exploded with part of my pancreas and intestines. 45 staples. Normally people do not live from this large of a perforation. All this from unending extremely high levels of stress worrying about my daughter 24/7.

Me, Mother, and Brother the Christmas we got the "Spirit Board" game. My Parents had no idea what they had done.

Me with a Favorite Horse

J. C. Story

CHAPTER 9

INVISIBLE MUSIC

Words are so very powerful, wouldn't you agree? Let's look at that, words and music—yet more powerful things that are invisible. I mean when you speak or sing words, they are pushed out into the air. Yes, you can hear words and music even though it is invisible. We can hear GOD/JESUS, too, even though HE is invisible, we hear HIM giving us advice deep inside ourselves, if we will only be still and quiet and concentrate on our deepest (sane & good) gut feeling—that's GOD/JESUS talking to you. One of the Biblical descriptions of GOD/JESUS' voice is as sounding like rushing waters, here are two Biblical verses:

Ezekiel 43:2 (NIV)
   "HIS [GOD] voice was like the roar of rushing waters."

Revelations 1:15 (NIV)
   "HIS [GOD] voice was like the sound of rushing waters."

There are many other examples in The Bible about

GOD/JESUS' voice as well. GOD/JESUS does actually speak words as well, mostly in crisis situations. I can't tell you how many stories I have heard about people being on the edge of some impending catastrophe when they hear a crystal clear, loud voice tell them what to do at the last minute (there's that last-minute thing again with GOD/JESUS). Here's one story told to me from the person it actually happened to. I will never forget this, a good Christian friend of mine who flies airplanes (not the psychotic attorney) was out having some fun in a small plane, flying down low to see close up, a certain pastureland, but when he pulled to go back high in the air something happened, causing him to lose control of one side of the plane. At the last minute he heard a clear loud voice from behind him (he was alone in the plane) telling him exactly what to do to save his own life and it worked! He said what the voice told him to do was a "pure genius" idea, and that he would have never thought of doing that, especially in the heat and stress of the moment. I hear these stories a lot when out on the streets talking to people about GOD/JESUS. Here's a well-known "mysterious voice" that saved a baby's life after her mom was killed in a car crash in a river. Lily Groesbeck (eighteen months old) survived all night, upside down, in a partially submerged car with her deceased mother in extremely cold weather. They had crashed and the mom had died on impact in March 2015. A fisherman found the wreckage the following day. Upon police's arrival, four different emergency officers heard a clearly adult voice from within the submerged car telling them to "help" the baby which could not be seen or heard because she was upside down (hiding her little body) with her car seat holding her right above the rushing river water. Prior to hearing that clear adult voice, the emergency team was about to start the process of towing the mangled wreckage out of the water (which would have killed the little baby stuck inside).

There have been many documentaries and true-story movies made about that Voice which saved someone's life at the last minute. So here, once again, I can compare GOD/JESUS to yet another invisible power, words and—by extension—music. We may not be able to see GOD/JESUS physically, however, HE is just as real as invisible music's power, and yes, we can hear HIM if we will really search HIM out. Be still and listen to what our soul is telling us deep down in our stomach, what you feel/hear from within yourself (the positive feelings and warnings of caution), that is GOD/JESUS' Voice.

Words and music are invisible unless you actually write them down. But still, in their original state of production, words and music are invisible. So again, we can understand something else extremely powerful being invisible. Much like how a text goes out into the air to reach someone's cell phone. You type those words into your phone then, when you press send, you are pushing those words out into the invisible, to be invisibly sent to someone. The power of words is invisible as well. For instance, "I love you" or "I hate you," either can be devastating, carrying the power of the world right to the pit of your stomach or your heart.

I am constantly bringing up invisible powers because people all over the world believe for a fact that everything invisible (which I've named throughout this book) are all very real facts that all the world has an absolute undeniable faith in.

Therefore, why is it so hard to understand GOD/JESUS and

HIS powers being invisible? We already know why HE must remain invisible, remember "waiting in line to see GOD!"

Think about this, mankind is just like the spoken word, in that before words are written down, they are simply invisible power. Before we were born, we were just like words, gravity, aerodynamics, carbon dioxide, oxygen, the wind, etc.—invisible power. Then our story was written in The Book of Life (which is mentioned all over The Bible). We were born and put into form, just like music and words are written down putting them into form. The Book of Life is talked about throughout The Bible from front to back, here are just a few places it is mentioned:

Psalm 69:28 (NIV)
> *May they be blotted out of **"The Book of Life"** and not listed with the righteous.*

Phillipians 4:3 (NIV)
> *Yes, and I ask you, my true companion, help these women since they have contented at my side in the cause of the gospel, along with Clement and the rest of my co-workers, whose names are in **"The Book of Life."***

Luke 10:20 (NIV)
> *However, do not rejoice that the spirits submit to you, but rejoice that your names are "Written in Heaven."*

Revelation 3:5 (NIV)
> *The one who is victorious will, like them, be dressed in white. I will never blot out the name of that person*

from ***"The Book of Life,"*** *but will acknowledge that name before MY FATHER and HIS Angels.*

Revelation 13:8 (NIV)

*All inhabitants of the earth will worship the beast—all whose names have not been written in **"The LAMB's Book of Life,"** The LAMB (JESUS) who was slain from the creation of the world.*

Revelation 17:8 (NIV)

*The beast, which you saw, once was, now is not, and yet will come up out of the abyss and go to its destruction. The inhabitants of the earth whose names have not been written in **"The Book of Life"** from the creation of the world will be astonished when they see the beast, because it once was, now is not, and yet will come.*

Revelation 20:12 (NIV)

*As I saw the dead, great and small, standing before the throne, and books were opened. Another book was opened, which is **"The Book of Life."** The dead were judged according to what they had done as recorded in the books.*

Revelation 20:15 (NIV)

*Anyone whose name was not found written in **"The Book of Life"** was thrown into the lake of fire.*

Revelation 21:27 (NIV)

Nothing impure will ever enter it, nor will anyone who

does what is shameful or deceitful, but only those whose names are written in **"The LAMB's (JESUS') Book of Life."**

Revelation 22:19 (NKJV)
And if anyone takes away from the words of the book of this prophecy, GOD shall take away his part from **"The Book of Life,"** *from the things which are written in this book.*

Invisible words rule the world through the mouths of presidents, leaders, and the like. GOD/JESUS rules the universe invisibly, then HE put HIMSELF down in form, just like putting words down in form when you write them on paper, JESUS is GOD put into human (flesh) form!

Everything I write about in this book is to get people to understand that it is possible for invisible things to exist, control, and even rule the very physical world around us. That just because something is invisible does not mean that it is not powerful and ever present. If all the aforementioned in this book from page one—if all those invisible powers are really real (and they are), then why can't GOD/JESUS be out there too? Like the powerful wind can create lighting, change landscapes, and even produce electricity via wind turbines.

Why is it so very hard for people to comprehend that the invisible things of the world and universe are in fact the most powerful, and more real, than most physical things that you can actually see?

Downloading GOD/JESUS into your soul is just as possible

as downloading music into the device of your choice. Just like music has the power to make you feel—good or bad or sad or lonely or happy or powerful or angry, etc.—GOD/JESUS can also make you feel things (mostly love) and empower you to achieve awesome things. However, if you want GOD/JESUS to empower you like music can, then you must first download HIM in order to be able to replay and pull on that invisible power, knowledge, love and forgiveness.

How many times have you heard a song that just gave you a powerful burst of energy which then propelled you through a great exercise session or got you through the rest of a day when you were simply exhausted? Please realize that song you heard is invisible, coming to you through the air. That song can only give you that burst of powerful energy if you LISTEN to it, correct? Likewise, GOD/JESUS' power can only give you HIS burst of power, knowledge, and love if you listen to HIM!

How can you feel anything from music you have never heard? Imagine if you had never heard your very favorite song in the whole world, the one song that gets your blood really pumping, and makes you feel extremely awesome.

That's what you're missing out on when you do not have GOD/JESUS in your life, that's why Christian's are out and about telling people left and right about HIM. Compare yourself, your favorite song of all time, and the way it makes you feel (remembering that it's invisible). What did you want to do the moment you heard it and felt the way it made you feel? You wanted to tell all your friends and anyone else who would listen, all about what an awesome (invisible) song you just heard. The thing that made you want to go tell everyone was the power surge you felt from it. You wanted everybody to feel that power too.

This is why Christian's, since CHRIST's resurrection, have been choosing even death (to be martyred) rather than to denounce HIS existence. They had lived a life feeling that power surge, accessing HIS knowledge, feeling HIS love and unconditional forgiveness all from GOD/JESUS since first having connected to HIS Wi-Fi, THE HOLY SPIRIT. That feel-good power surge GOD/JESUS puts out is much, much, much more powerful and euphoric than your favorite song. Hence the overwhelming willingness by millions upon millions to die brutal deaths rather than be without GOD/JESUS. That power-surge feeling is wisdom, love, ecstasy—every good feeling under the sun all rolled into one, and it's constantly streaming into you when you accept GOD/JESUS' Wi-Fi.

Think about the twenty-one Christian men who were beheaded on that Libyan beach in 2015. They had been given a choice to deny JESUS and they would have been set free, no problem. Why then, did they refuse to deny JESUS CHRIST, why? All twenty-one men refused their freedom on those terms, at which point they were each beheaded—on camera! The video was then released to the internet and is still there today. From this we know that people are still dying for CHRIST JESUS to this very day. So, understand that people dying for faith in GOD/JESUS is not some situation that happened during Biblical times alone, it is alive, well, and ongoing right now, unfortunately. Why would millions in this day and time still continue to choose death rather than deny CHRIST JESUS? Because they had connected themselves to

HIS Wi-Fi and experienced a very real relationship with GOD/JESUS and they clearly understood that physical death was only a transportation of the soul from earth to heaven!

Look at this, all those millions of millions of people for the past two thousand years have been easily willing to die brutal deaths for some reason. They cannot all be crazy or delusional, there are far too many martyrs for CHRIST JESUS throughout history to be a lie—the Roman Arena is proof of that. There are two billion with a "b", that's *two billion* Christians worldwide today (actually 2.3 billion), they can't all be crazy!

On the few occasions when I do listen to secular, invisible music, I find myself singing the love songs to GOD/JESUS. Or receive them as if HE is sending it to me. I am constantly fitting GOD/JESUS into all music I hear because the reality is that HE created it in the first place. Now, what we do to pervert invisible music is on mankind.

There's a couple of secular songs I've heard on secular radio that describe how GOD/JESUS feels about us all. One is called "Get Closer" by Seals & Crofts (1976). You really need to hear it, so go right now, look it up on the internet and watch/listen to the video with lyrics, if possible. Your train of thought should be that this is GOD/JESUS singing straight to you. You can do this with a lot of secular music. The last thing about this song I want to call your attention to is that there is a verse in The Bible which sums up this exact song: James 4:8 "Come near to GOD and HE will come near to you" (NIV Bible). The other song that comes to mind is "To Love Somebody" by Bee Gees (1967). These two songs I have named here, when you listen to them, hear them as if

GOD/JESUS was singing directly to you, and you alone. None of these songs were written with GOD/JESUS in mind, as far as I know, but when I listen to non-Christian music, I hear it as love to or from my MAKER! Right now I am facing a life or death situation due to my immune system crashing. My doctors can't figure out why so my prognosis is not good. When I think about my own possible impending death, Shakira's song "Whenever, Wherever" (2001) comes to mind. I am ready whenever my LOVE, my ALL, my GOD/JESUS wants me home. When I think about that day, I want to go dancing before the LORD like King David did in the Bible: 2 Samuel 6:14! When I say "I love HIM", I mean HE is the ONLY ONE for me for all eternity, I would dance for HIM forever and serve HIM forever until the very end of time because I have already been there & back so I know.

Last but not least, I want to tell you a story about the musical director in heaven. He, himself actually built of all the musical instruments you have ever heard of. This being's entire body and all body parts were made up of musical instruments, all the one's you have heard of and many more you have not. Let me introduce Lucifer (which means light), the name satan—the devil—had had before his great fall from grace. Besides his body being actually made up entirely of musical instruments, he was also covered on the outside with every jewel and beautiful stone ever in existence.

The inside of his being parts were actual shiny instruments made up of pure precious materials, such as gold and silver, covered (in place of skin) with diamonds, jewels, etc. The description of satan I am speaking of is from The Bible:

Ezekiel 28:13-16 (NKJV Bible)
> *"You were in Eden, the garden of GOD; Every precious stone was your covering: The sardius, topaz, and diamond, beryl, onyx, and jasper, sapphire, turquoise, and emerald with gold. The workmanship of your timbrels and pipes was prepared for you on the day you were created. You were the anointed cherub who covers; I established you; you were on the holy mountain of GOD; you walked back and forth in the midst of fiery stones. You were perfect in your ways from the day you were created, till iniquity was found in you. By the abundance of your trading you became filled with violence within, and you sinned; therefore I cast you as a profane thing out of the mountain of GOD; and I destroyed you, o covering cherub, from the midst of the fiery stones."*

He was the top, bar none, of all music in heaven. Lucifer was created and set right next to GOD/JESUS, he was fantastically gorgeous and so beautiful it would actually kill any human to look upon him as he was.

Ezekiel 28:17 (MSG)
> *"Your beauty went to your head. You corrupted wisdom by using it to get worldly fame. I threw you to the ground, sent you sprawling before an audience of kings and let them gloat over your demise."*

This being was—without a doubt—absolutely, amazingly awesome! He was the master of all music throughout the universe.

I tell you all of this because music has power to influence you, as I mentioned before, and satan still has access to that power. Have you ever been really angry and then heard a song that pushed you over the edge, to the point where you wanted to go take physical revenge? Before the song played, you were angry but under control, then you heard that song and all of a sudden, the urge to attack the perpetrator of your pain became uncontrollable. Like everything else, there is a good and a bad side, the same is true with music. There are thousands of people in jail and prisons all over the world because of one song (invisible power) that pushed them over the edge to go get physical. My point is that—like drugs or alcohol/spirits—music can also be a tool satan uses to trip you up. After all, satan was the original controller of all music. He was the worship/music leader of all the heavens, it stands to reason that he is very skilled at using it today.

I used to listen to "advisory" (warning) type music. Now thinking back, that music fueled me much further down the wrong road than I had ever planned on going. I still remember my emotions prior to getting into my car and turning that music on. I was emotional but I was still in control, then after listening to a few of those foul language songs, I became so angry that I did things I still regret to this day. Satan had influenced me without my knowledge or permission. He had taken control of my course of life for that day, and the ripple effects from that were like dominos falling on others around me. Please be aware of the influential power of music you listen to, it can be like a drug, making you feel good in the moment but the repercussions are a living hell!

As for me, I learned the hard way not to listen to anything

with advisory warnings ever! Now and then, I will be searching music in the car and stop on one of those "advisory" songs for just a moment. Before I know it, those aggressive feelings start to bubble up inside me again. As soon as I change it back to Christian rock, rap, etc., within minutes, I can feel a major difference in my mood and decision making.

I have become so sensitive to satan's power to play with our emotions (through invisible words/songs) that I rarely listen to any music or TV that is not Christian. Whether it is a movie, talk show, or whatever, satan destroyed the lives of my loved ones, as well as my own, and I will never let my guard down again. It would blow your mind to see how different your emotional state of being would be if you did a trial of "Christian only" entertainment with no outside influences whatsoever, for only a thirty-day trial. There's a Christian, nation-wide radio station named K-LOVE. They have something called "The K-LOVE Challenge" which is to take thirty days of Christian-ONLY entertainment, then see how you're feeling after the thirty days. Thousands are reporting major positive changes after taking the thirty-day challenge. Always remember, satan started out as music himself, he *was* music, he didn't just produce music or create it, but he embodied music, it came from within his very being, his breath was music—so beware of satan using music to hack into your soul and take control of you. Or the next thing you know, you could be waking up in prison, hooked on drugs or any number of horrific problems.

Let me ask you this, how many people do you think committed murder, injected heroin (for the first time), beat someone (beyond recognition), or planned a robbery to the tune of some influentially powerful music? How many people commit suicide to one of those "advisory" songs pushing them to it? It happens every single day. Invisible music has very real powers which can lift you up to heaven or drag you down to hell. Please be careful what music you feed your soul! Here are a few examples of Christian rap, rock, and contemporary songs for you to consider in place of those "advisory" songs. Christian music can blow your mind in a very positive way so give it a listen. The songs below are not in any kind of order and there are many more absolutely power-charged songs I didn't list so please do an in-depth search on all Christian music. These songs are simply an example to get you started. Enjoy!!!!!!!!!!!!!!!!!!!!!!!!!!!!!!

1. Andy Mineo: "You Can't Stop Me" (Rap/Hard Rock) Andy Mineo is actually telling satan (in this song), he can't stop him!
2. Passion Conferences: "Glorioso Dia" (En Espanol)
3. Crowder: "Lift Your Head Weary Sinner" (Southern Rock)
4. Lauren Daigle: "Still Rolling Stones" (Soul/Contemporary)
5. for KING & COUNTRY: "TOGETHER" (Pop/Contemporary)
6. Jesse Fisher: "Good News" (My Favorite Rap)
7. We The Kingdom: "Holy Water" (Soul/Contemporary)
8. Maverick City Music: "The Story I'll Tell"

(Absolutely Angelically Beautiful-Above & Beyond Any Category) I pray this will be sung @ my funeral!
9. Casting Crowns: "Nobody" (Contemporary)
10. Third Day: "Revelation" filmed @ Salvation Mountain, Official Music Video (Southern Rock)
11. Maverick City Music & UPPERROOM: "I thank GOD" (Pop)
12. Elevation Worship: "Lo Haras Otra Vez" (En Espanol)
13. Elevation Worship: "Might Get Loud" (Rock/Rap)

CHAPTER 10

THE STORY OF LUCIFER, SATAN THE HACKER

Here is what happened in heaven and why there is so much pain and suffering in the world. Understanding how I had explained earlier about The Bible telling us everything we will ever need to know about navigating through this world. The Bible is the map on how to survive in the flesh but also after the body has passed away also. Kind of like in *Jumanji: Welcome to the Jungle (2017)* where they had a map, The Bible is your map. Just like most movies of that nature, like *Raiders of The Lost Ark (1981)* (the lost ark is what holds GOD's Ten Commandments), they had clues for direction. They always had to figure out what the clues were because the clues for their directions were not spelled out much of the time. Hidden within the words and clues (if you paid close attention), then you could decipher how to navigate to the goal (figure out how GOD/JESUS says to solve your problem).

Note: To have a portion of The Bible deciphered for you on video, within a few hours, please go to the internet and watch *The Harbinger Decoded* (2013) documentary by Johnathan Cahn (it's free to watch on YouTube, or you may purchase the DVD). Make sure you view the Johnathan Cahn "Harbinger Decoded" of 2013 production date because Johnathan Cahn has produced other more recent shows. You need to see his very first documentary to understand his latter one's. "The Harbinger Decoded" (2013) deciphers what happened on 9/11 and what America is headed for now, showing you where it was in The Bible. This guy is absolutely super intelligent, he can blow away anyone who thinks they're too cool for school! Johnathan Cahn's information is deciphered from The Bible and GOD/JESUS' Wi-Fi. It's a MUST SEE!

The Bible is made up of two parts, the Old Testament and the New Testament, the entire book is your map of clues and GOD/JESUS has laid it out twice for you. The New Testament is simply the Old Testament revealed or described in an updated manor for the time right after GOD/JESUS came to earth to live with us, JESUS in the flesh. I know it still seems complicated even in the New Testament. Still, compared to the Old Testament, the New Testament really was written so that people of GOD/JESUS' day (in the flesh) could get a good understanding even if they were not educated. That is why GOD/JESUS (in the flesh) would tell them stories (parables), in order to help them and us to understand HIS navigation map as it were.

At any rate, here is satan's story from throughout the entire Bible, Old and New Testament. Some of the following Biblical verses are being repeated from earlier due to there importance in helping your understanding.

Revelations 12:7–12 (MSG)

> "War broke out in Heaven. Michael and his Angels fought the Dragon. The Dragon and his angels fought back, but were no match for Michael. They were cleared out of Heaven, not a sign of them left. The great Dragon—ancient serpent, the one called devil and satan, the one who led the whole earth astray—thrown out, and all his angels thrown out with him, thrown down to earth. Then I heard a strong voice out of Heaven saying,
>
> Salvation and power are established! Kingdom of our GOD, authority of HIS MESSIAH [JESUS]! The Accuser of our brothers and sisters thrown out, who accused them day and night before GOD. They defeated him through the BLOOD OF THE LAMB [JESUS' BLOOD] and the bold word of their witness [our testimony to others]. They weren't in love with themselves; they were willing to die for CHRIST. So rejoice, O Heavens, and all who live there, but doom to earth and sea, for the devil's come down on you with both feet; he's had a great fall; he's wild and raging with anger; he hasn't much time and he knows it!"

Isaiah 14:12–17 (MSG)

> "What a comedown this, O Babylon! Daystar! Son of Dawn!
> Flat on your face in the underworld mud, you, famous for flattening nations! You said to yourself, "I'll climb to Heaven. I'll set my throne over the stars of GOD. I'll run the assembly of angels that meets on sacred

Mount Zaphon. I'll climb to the top of the clouds. I'll take over as King of the Universe!"

But you didn't make it, did you? Instead of climbing up, you came down—down with the underground dead. Down to the abyss of the Pit. People will stare and muse: "Can this be the one who terrorized earth and its kingdoms, turned earth to a moonscape, wasted its cities, shut up his prisoners to a living death?"

Ezekiel 28:11–19 (MSG)

"You had everything going for you. You were in Eden, GOD's garden. You were dressed in splendor, your robe studded with jewels: carnelian, peridot, and moonstone, beryl, onyx, and jasper, sapphire, turquoise, and emerald, all in settings of engraved gold. A robe was prepared for you the same day you were created. You were the anointed Cherub. I placed you on the mountain of GOD. You strolled in magnificence among the stones of fire. From the day of your creation you were sheer perfection . . . and then imperfection—evil!—was detected in you. In much buying and selling you turned violent, you sinned! I threw you, disgraced, off the mountain of GOD. I threw you out—you, the anointed angel—Cherub. No more strolling among the gems of fire for you!
YOUR BEAUTY WENT TO YOUR HEAD!
You corrupted wisdom by using it to get worldly fame. I threw you to the ground, sent you sprawling before an audience of kings and let them gloat over your demise. By sin after sin after sin, by your corrupt ways of doing

business, you defiled your holy places of worship [music]. So, I set a fire around and within you. It burned you up. I reduced you to ashes. All anyone sees now when they look at you is ashes, a pitiful mound of ashes. All who once knew you now throw up their hands:
'This can't have happened!'
'THIS HAS HAPPENED!'"

Luke 10:18–20 (MSG)

"JESUS said, 'I know, I saw satan fall, like a bolt of lightning out of the sky. See what I've given you? Safe passage as you walk on snakes and scorpions, and protection from every assault of the Enemy. No one can put a hand on you. All the same, the great triumph is not in your authority over evil, but in GOD's authority over you and presence with you [GOD's WI-FI]. Not what you do for GOD but what GOD does for you—that's the agenda for rejoicing.'"

1 Peter 5:8–11 (MSG)

"Keep a cool head. Stay alert. The devil is poised to pounce, and would like nothing better than to catch you napping. Keep your guard up. You're not the only ones plunged into these hard times. It's the same with Christians all over the world. So keep a firm grip on the faith. The suffering won't last forever. It won't be long before this generous GOD who has great plans for us in CHRIST—eternal and glorious plans they are!—will have you put together and on your feet for good. HE gets the last word; yes, HE does!"

Look at this example of how The Bible is a map of clues that can be taken at face value but also can be deciphered to comprehend it's deeper, secondary meaning. I will explain The Bible verse below.

Revelations 12:1–2 (MSG)
> *"A great Sign appeared in Heaven: A Woman dressed all in sunlight, standing on the moon, and crowned with Twelve Stars. She was giving birth to a Child and cried out in the pain of childbirth."*

Explanation: The Woman described is actually Israel, and the Twelve Stars are actually The Twelve Tribes of Israel. The Child she was giving birth to is CHRIST JESUS.

Here's another part of that chapter I will show you the verse and then explain it.

Revelations 12:5–6 (MSG)
> *"The Woman gave birth to a SON who will shepherd all nations with an iron rod. Her SON was seized and placed safely before GOD on HIS throne. The Woman herself escaped to the desert to a place of safety prepared by GOD, all comforts provided her for 1,260 days."*

Explanation: The SON is JESUS and yes, HE was seized (murdered/crucified), at which point HE went back to be with GOD. Also, we know that the Woman is Israel which is of course in the desert, Israel, the Promise Land, which GOD had prepared and given to Israel thousands of years ago and now with "the iron dome" Israel (in the desert) is safe.

Jewish people today are escaping persecution from all over the world by going back to Israel (the desert) to wait.

Look, I mean this stuff is better than any video game or mystery to figure out because it is for real, for real (tip my hat to Pastor Tony Evans, for real-for real, he's the bomb! Check out Tony Evans sermon, "Purpose of Detours" on the internet, twenty-eight minutes).

Remember just how many invisible powers control the world. Now with that understanding and thought process, apply that understanding to GOD/JESUS' Wi-Fi and satan the hacker. Mankind understands and studies the invisible powers of the world such as the wind, carbon dioxide, aerodynamics, etc., so that we will understand how to best access their respective powers for the best benefits.

Example, back to aerodynamics, you must first study this invisible power and learn all about its benefits, pros, and cons before you just jump into an airplane and start trying to fly, right? Once you have learned how to use the invisible—yet life changing—power of aerodynamics, then you can fly an airplane with the knowledge that the invisible powers of aerodynamics will help and benefit you. Your body and life are like that airplane, so you really do not want to go flying through your life without the knowledge of how to navigate toward life and not death. In other words, if you were to go up and try to fly an airplane without the knowledge of the invisible forces which will be coming against your plane then you will defiantly crash and burn. Like so many people today who start out in life speeding toward success (like I had done) then they crash and burn (like I did), why? Because we were flying our planes (bodies) without the knowledge of the invisible forces coming against us, namely satan the hacker. Going through life being defiant to GOD/JESUS' universal laws (the Ten Commandments & The Bible) will only end in the same way that flying a plane without respecting the laws of aerodynamics will end, which is in much pain and suffering if not an early death.

We can all agree that there is good and evil in the world. It would stand to reason that before we get our big game plan on, we had better have the full knowledge of what our oppositions will be. Evil, satan the hacker, that is your opposition. If you are not prepared with spiritual cyber protection—GOD/JESUS—it is only a matter of time before you hit that brick wall described earlier (chapter two) in Oxford's aerodynamics description: "the plane has the aerodynamics of a brick once the forward thrust is lost" (Oxford Languages Descriptive Sentence).

Please do not do what I and my ex-husband did, we called ourselves Christians but never opened our Bible to study one word and so we crashed and burned, taking our innocent daughter with us. Go to the internet and look up Pastor Jentzen Franklin's sermon, "Little by Little." That sermon describes what happened to me in summary and why I crashed and burned! Jentzen Franklin is another one of those cool pastors, he can play a saxophone like nobody's business too!

Back to the story of satan, right now he is traveling the earth, looking at all of our sins and then zooming back up to heaven to accuse you and me before GOD/JESUS, day and night. If you have no connection with GOD/JESUS then there is nothing GOD/JESUS can do to protect you from satan and so HE has no choice but to let satan have you. Here's an example from The Bible:

Job 1:6–7 (MSG)
> *"One day when the Angels came to report to GOD, satan, who was the designated Accuser, came along with them. GOD singled out satan and said, 'What have you been up to?'*
> *Satan answered GOD, 'Going here and there, checking things out on earth.'"*

Here is the situation we are up against (the invisible situation coming at us all). The hacker satan is still allowed limited access into heaven mainly to spew insults about us right into GOD/JESUS' face. Because satan is jealous of GOD/JESUS' love for humanity, satan is always up there telling all of the bad things we are doing down here on earth.

Example: Like when you are dating a new person and you are both so happy. The person you had been involved with before is now calling you every single time they get dirt on your new love, all in order to tell you about it in the hopes you will leave your new love/relationship.

That is what The Bible verse above is describing. How, you may ask, does satan get to keep going into heaven at all? Let me describe it like this: if GOD/JESUS were to kill satan or completely disintegrate any remembrance of him, then that would destroy "free will." All heavenly and earthly beings would be so frightened of GOD/JESUS possibly disintegrating them that they would be too scared NOT to love GOD/JESUS. Again, who wants forced love? Therefore, satan lives for now, he was seriously demoted but yes, he still has some access to GOD/JESUS temporarily. This temporary access is in order for GOD/JESUS to prove to all other beings that "free will" does exist. That everyone has a choice to want to be with GOD/JESUS or not. That we will not be disintegrated if we chose NOT to be with GOD/JESUS. This, however, is not a permanent situation. Because instead of receiving discipline humbly, satan only made things much worse by taking possession of Judas. Next, satan advised the police where JESUS was located which is when the police seized JESUS, beat HIM, and crucified HIM. So not only did satan challenge GOD/JESUS in heaven but then he did it again on earth! Yet GOD/JESUS still allows satan to live—all because if HE did not then all heavenly and earthly beings would be too scared NOT to love GOD/JESUS. In other words, satan must be allowed to live (for now) so that we are assured of "free will."

Luke 22:3 (NIV)
> *"Then satan entered Judas, surnamed Iscariot, who was numbered among the twelve."*

After satan caused JESUS to be murdered, satan's destiny was sealed, doomed for a certain point in time when he will be permanently bound in the lake of fire.

Revelations 20:10 (TLV)
> *"And the devil who deceived them was thrown into the lake of fire and brimstone, where the beast and the false prophet are too, and they shall be tortured day and night forever and ever."*

Did you know that after satan left Judas' body (once he

had delivered JESUS to HIS executioner's) Judas then came to his senses and realized what he had done (while being hacked by satan) and committed suicide?

Matthew 27:3–5 (MSG)
> *"Judas, the one who betrayed HIM, realized that JESUS was doomed. Overcome with remorse, he gave back the thirty silver coins to the high priests, saying, 'I've sinned. I've betrayed an innocent man.' They said, 'What do we care? That's your problem!' Judas threw the silver coins into the Temple and left. Then he went out and hung himself!"*

For now, the hacker of souls is still cruising all around the entire earth, always looking for any weakness in us so that he may hack into our spiritual receivers. The devil wants to pull a master identity theft or at the very least, infect us with a virus. He then leaves this virus (evil thoughts) within us to start the infection so that he can come back later. After the virus has weakened us severely (growing those evil thoughts & piling up evil actions), it will make it much easier to completely take over our lives. Make no mistake, you cannot beat satan the hacker without GOD/JESUS. The devil is unbeatable from our human bodies and without The Creator of us both. Look at this description (from The Bible) of satan's strength.

Job 41:5–26 (TLV)
> *"Who can strip off his outer garment? Who can penetrate his double armor? Who can open the doors of*

his face, ringed with fearsome teeth? His rows of shields are his pride, shut up closely as with tight seal; each so close to the next, that no air can pass between. They are joined one to another; they clasp each other and cannot be separated. He sneezes out light; his eyes are like the eyelids of dawn. Out of his mouth go flames, sparks of fire shoot out. Smoke pours from his nostrils, as a boiling pot over burning reeds. His breath sets coals ablaze and flames dart from his mouth. Strength resides in his neck; dismay runs before him. The folds of his flesh are tightly joined; they are firm on him, immovable. His heart is hard as rock, hard as a lower millstone. When he rises up, the mighty are afraid; at his crashing they retreat. A sword that reaches him has no effect – nor with a spear, dart, or javelin. He regards iron as straw, bronze as rotten wood. Arrows do not make him flee; sling stones become like chaff to him. A club is regarded as stubble; he laughs at the rattling of a lance. His undersides are jagged potsherds, leaving a trail like a threshing sledge in mud. He makes the deep boil like a cauldron and stirs up the sea like a pot of ointment. He leaves a shining wake behind him; one would think the deep had white hair. Nothing on dry land is equal—a creature without fear. He sees every haughty thing; he is king over all who are proud".

This hacker, satan, is the ultimate badass. People with much pride are satan's favorite because he can bait them with their own greed.

However, GOD/JESUS is an absolute master at flipping things on satan. What I mean is that GOD/JESUS can take a horrible situation—like JESUS on the cross, dripping blood and in horrific pain for hours—and turn it so that it backfires on satan. Look at satan hacking into Judas to get JESUS murdered. Please recognize how GOD caused it to backfire on satan. Because of JESUS' death on the cross, humanity can now be saved if we so choose to be. If we accept JESUS' pure death (HIS falsely accused compensation) for our sins. Or in other words, JESUS' false imprisonment (torture and death) gained him trillions of dollars which HE has chosen to give away as credit for our sins!

We can do the same thing to satan that GOD/JESUS has done (with HIS Wi-Fi connection). Make whatever satan has done to you backfire on him, that is the ultimate invisible power!

What do you think I have done in writing this book? I am causing everything satan did to me and to my daughter, to backfire on him, boomerang back on satan, flip the situation on that jerk! Shiitake mushrooms and amen, where's the Tylenol!

The devil took over my life and caused me to do wretched things (which is a whole other book), in that during all my trials and tribulations I was the equivalent to a drowning person—grabbing and grasping at everyone to stay a-float in a complete panic, only instead of the ones I grabbed keeping me above water, I only pulled them down with me. But after all was said and done, instead of cringing and hiding, hoping no one finds out, I confess all my sins out in public whenever I am talking to people. I use my testimony so that they know anybody can be saved, no matter what they have done, even murder (which I have done also in the aforementioned abortion).

I have broken every one of the Ten Commandments, repeatedly harming others in the process. I tell them all to broken people on the streets. Once I am finished telling them just how wretched I was; then they see hope in their own lives to turn from their sins (spiritual cyber virus infections). This is how you can flip those shiitake mushrooms on satan the hacker.

If you are known for rolling with satan, in that you are participating in something which you know is seriously bad then STOP doing it immediately! Just freaking stop!

Get to know GOD/JESUS' power, bar none, learn like you would learn aerodynamics invisible powers before flying a jet. Then get out in the world and flip the snot out of the situation satan has defaulted you into! Boomerang him good by sending everything he did to you, back on to him. You do that by stealing souls from him, by going out and telling people all your sins and how GOD/JESUS forgave you and on top of that, gave you this awesome invisible power, stronger than any hurricane-force wind!

Psalm 107:2 (NIV)
"Let the redeemed of the Lord tell their story—those HE redeemed from the hand of the foe (satan)."

Instead of spending your time and energy trying to get revenge on all the different people who have caused you pain (which is exactly what satan wants you to do). Focus instead on the true enemy, satan the hacker! Just remember that picture of the devil, sitting back in his recliner, laughing his ass off at you. All while you huff and puff, getting all upset at some other poor soul whom satan has played as well. I don't know about you, but I seriously hate when the one who caused my suffering is laughing at my pain. Those people you want to take revenge on are victims of the devil just exactly like you are. Get this straight and crystal clear, 100 percent understand that people are not your enemy or your problem, satan is! I've repeated myself here because it's that important.

The last thing I want to notify you of is that satan is a being of light, a servant of light, and the ruler of the kingdom of the air.

2 Corinthians 11:14 (NIV)
"And no wonder, for satan himself masquerades as 'an angel of light'".

Ephesians 2:2 (NIV)
"In which you used to live when you followed the ways of this world and 'the ruler of the kingdom of the air', the spirit who is now at work in those who are disobedient".

Knowing these things, considering that satan masquerades as an angel of light and he is the ruler of the kingdom of the air. You can then conclude that it is not a stretch to consider that there is the possibility of no aliens or UFOs, but demons and satan masquerading as such. The devil does this to cause any form of doubt at all toward the existence of GOD/JESUS. Demons pretending to be UFOs and aliens, this has been a topic of discussion since Biblical days. It is completely possible that demons are what we are seeing in the skies zooming about as a light. Yes, I believe the stories of people being abducted. Because I understand that what could actually have abducted them were not aliens but demons. This is nothing new, demons have been abducting people since Noah's time which is why the flood was necessary. The offspring of those demon abductions had to be wiped off the face of the earth. They were so extremely corrupt and evil, hence the flood and Noah's ark.

Genesis 6:2 (NLT)
"The sons of GOD saw the beautiful women and 'took' any they wanted . . ."

The "sons of GOD" which are earth bound here in this verse is referring to satan's crew that got kicked out of heaven with satan. They were sons of GOD until they decided to follow satan.

If you would like more information on the subject of aliens and demons, please see the documentary film "Alien Intrusion: Unmasking A Deception" (2018) Hosted by John Schneider.

The most amazing thing about this film's studies are the interviews with people who have actually been abducted then screamed out the name of JESUS at which point the aliens (demons) fled rapidly and the person was freed.

Last but not least, let me suggest an answer to the question of what happened to the dinosaurs? The Bible tells us about satan being thrown out of heaven and down like lighting; could it be satan and his crew that hit the earth causing the death of all dinosaurs and the ice age (not a meteorite)? Angelic beings are huge! Just food for thought. Again, I will urgently suggest the series "Creation In The 21st Century" by David Rives, which interviews top Scientist and Archaeologist in explaining the latest in the unreliability of some forms of certain carbon dating and many other unreliable factors that the evolutionist depends upon.

Also let's answer the question of how old the earth is. Our instruction manual, The Bible, tells us, "A thousand years is like a day and a day is like a thousand years in GOD/JESUS' realm.

Psalm 90:4 (TLV)
"For a thousand years in YOUR sight are like a day just passing by, or like a watch in the night."

2 Peter 3:8 (TLV)
"But don't forget this one thing, loved ones, that with the LORD one day is like a thousand years, and a thousand years are like one day."

CHAPTER 11

STOP—BE STILL
(Psalm 46:10)

"Step out of the traffic! Take a long, loving look at ME, your HIGH GOD, above politics, above everything."
(MSG Psalm 46:10)

"HE says, 'Be still, and know that I AM GOD!'"
(Psalm 46:10 NIV)

In other words, be still and get to know GOD/JESUS, take some time to read, study and learn The Truth which is JESUS, The Way, The Truth & The Life.

Nothing worth having is ever easy, anything worth having is going to be hard work. This much, I am sure, you will agree with. When people want to live in mansions, with a nice size savings account, and an even fuller checking account, garage stocked with nice cars, etc. What then, do they do in order to achieve such goals? For starters, they get educated in the field of work with which they will rely on. The type of education needed for such high goals will be extensive and take a minimum of four years (if not more) of reading, studying, and being tested on the subject with which they will be depending upon to supply all that they desire.

This is a given, and is completely accepted by all the world, correct? Now we know that throughout all those years of learning, studying, reading, rereading, and being tested, there will be very hard times, even exhausting. People push through all of those trials and tribulations, pain and suffering, because they understand, without a doubt, that this is what must be endured in order to achieve their ultimate goals.

Now compare peace, joy, happiness, love, financial stability, and a calm atmospheric-globe-like force field surrounding you. Wherever you go, you're protected; compare that to all the aforementioned wealth, mansions, prestige, and cars. However, in this comparison, understand that if you have the mansion, etc., this goal achieved will not bring with it peace, joy, happiness, and love. In other words, you would have all the material things, but those things, do not a happy home, make! Look at one of many of those wealthy, sports figures that went rogue and murdered people, for example. You can see pictures of all their wealth, cars, and beautiful mansions, some even wearing a cross around their neck (which does nothing without GOD/JESUS' daily Wi-Fi connection), however as beautiful as their mansions were, they had no peace, joy, or happiness. All of their material possessions, in the end, where just bait for satan. The devil, like any baited, aggressive animal, came running and devoured everything, including the people themselves.

Before you do anything in life, you must make up your mind what you really want. Peace, joy, happiness, and love, or a mansion full of demons? If you choose the mansion and wealth scenario, first and foremost, right out of the gate, then you are almost guaranteed not to attain any kind of lasting peace, true love, or happiness (this is why had mentioned John McAfee earlier). However, if you want the peace and happiness, they should be obtained first (whenever possible), before you acquire anything else material (a.k.a. bait for the devil).

Now, the only way to attain the true peace and happiness I speak of is to understand all the invisible powers and forces around you first. In the same way you would learn aerodynamics first before flying a jet. Those invisible powers control the peace and happiness on earth, just like invisible oxygen controls all life on earth. Here's where my next comparison comes in, for true peace, love, and happiness. Just like college for a career, you must study the invisible powers, learn all about what you are dealing with in life, GOD/JESUS and satan the hacker. Many people would say that peace, true love, and happiness are worth more than all the money in the world. There are many multi-millionaires and even billionaires who have committed suicide because they had everything material but no peace or true love, only loneliness, no happiness whatsoever.

That being said, you can clearly understand that no one in the entire world can purchase a lasting, atmospheric-globe-like force field of peace and calm, which surrounds them at all times. That atmospheric globe of peaceful contentment within any circumstance is what I now have 24/7.

No amount of money can buy that, yet you can achieve it. It is available but not for sale. To acquire this priceless, life-long, invisible protection will take hard work, physical sacrifice, and much testing. I should know because I have finally, finally attained it myself.

You must put yourself through an education of self-discipline, a course which will bring you to your knees at times. There will be much sacrifice, pain, suffering, and exhaustion. Last but not least, testing, you will be tested over and over, just like you were going through four years of college to earn a certain degree. Except these tests will be spiritual, in the form of life's trials & tribulations.

The OWNER and CREATOR of peace, love, and happiness (all invisible yet everyone wants them) is of course, the same ONE who created the universe, GOD/JESUS. HE has all of the joy, peace, and love available to us all at any time, however all of the aforementioned are attached to GOD/JESUS and it is impossible to separate these coveted items from HIM. Therefore, you must attain a relationship with GOD/JESUS in order to really enjoy your life to the extent that is possible. Much like in *Raiders of The Lost Ark (1981)*, you must follow a map of directions (The Bible) to attain these goals. The journey will not be easy, but it will be well worth all the effort you can muster, with the same effort you would put into a college education.

The approach to this journey will be to first stop everything and anything that you are doing which you know is not right. I mean just absolutely stop it, immediately.

(Note: If you are dealing with chemical addictions, you must slowly stop one at a time. I slowly weaned myself off one addiction at a time and I had several severe addictions. You may want to check yourself into a Christian rehabilitation center like the ones Mike Lindell offers nationwide, for free. Please buy all "My Pillow" products when possible, as those products fund the free rehabilitation facilities Mike Lindell offers).

What I mean by stopping everything you know is wrong: Say if you are having sex outside of marriage, just stop, or if you are always gossiping, just stop, etc. Like Psalm 46:10 (NLT) says, "Be still and know that I AM GOD." Now see what I mean about this way being like college, it involves great sacrifice. Like anything really worth having, it is well worth all the great peace, love, and happiness you will obtain in the end, if you hang in there and do not give up!

Galatians 6:9 (TLV)
"So let us not lose heart in doing good, for in due time we will reap if we don't give up!" (Remember "reaping" what we sow.)

Just stop doing things that make your own stomach turn. You know when you are doing something wrong, so just STOP! By the way, about not having sex before marriage, see if this train of thought may help you to understand just how powerful sex is: It is the way an actual human being is made! It stands to reason, something that powerful should be respected, and therefore reserved for after marriage only. Plus, if someone is willing to date you for a minimum of one full year (before marriage) without any sexual relations at all, that will confirm you have a much greater chance they will stick with you through the ups and downs of a lifelong marriage. And do not go get married right after you meet someone just to have sex, because I promise you, it will not work! GOD/JESUS is ever watchful, and HE cannot be deceived! Just so you know, I personally have chosen to live a celibate life in dedication to GOD/JESUS' work. I've been living this way for more than seven years now and am completely happy, though I am not suggesting this lifestyle to anyone, only to abstain from sexual contact until marriage or remarriage (if your divorced), it's never too late to start over.

That being said, the next thing that will probably happen is that you will find yourself alone much more than before. This is where you start your study courses toward your degree for peace, joy, love, and your calm, atmospheric-globe-like force field. This degree will be with you for the rest of your life and carry you into a wonderful eternity even after death.

Get into The Bible and get seriously serious as you would if you were studying for a physician's license, law degree or pilot's license. In the same way you would attend college courses for so many hours per day, then do the same with GOD/JESUS. Learning your way to true success by figuring out the direction map GOD/JESUS has left us which is your Bible. When you are not reading The Bible then take a course by turning on Trinity Broadcasting Network, Christian TV or internet. For starters, watch my list of Christian films & shows in the back of this book. Approach it with notebook in hand to write down anything that catches your attention or grabs you, then (just like college) use your daily notes to look up or study what you wrote. I cannot stress enough that you should watch *The Harbinger Decoded* (2013) by Johnathan Cahn, it can be viewed free on Youtube. This really should be what you start your journey through The Bible with. It will jump-start your understanding of The Bible and its hidden meanings.

Listen, don't look at Christian TV as just being preached to, those pastors, like college professors, are explaining how to navigate The Bible and the invisible realm that controls what happens to you on a daily basis. That is your road map to lasting peace and true happiness, so listen to them. Rewatch sermons over and over if you get the chance, because you will get a new understanding each time. Rereading The Bible also will show you something new every time, I read a different version of The Bible every single year and every time, I discover something else I never understood before.

As you go, GOD/JESUS will start to download understanding and wisdom into your very soul. HE will continue with more and more downloads as you move forward. Attending the University of GOD/JESUS (within yourself) will be the biggest challenge of your life. For this reason, there are so many miserable, lonely people in the world who simply refuse to try or listen (which used to be me until the suffering became unbearable). Read a bit of your Bible every single day whether your flesh likes it or not!

Just like obtaining a law degree takes years of time and extreme dedication, it is well worth it all to have happiness and peace. The great difference between obtaining a law degree and a peace and happiness degree is that the peace and happiness degree is free (financially speaking). However, it will cost you in friends (the bad influences), sex relations outside of marriage (gotta' go), drugs, excessive drinking, and your time and attention. Here's an example of why your bad-influence friends and sex partners must go. You can actually do this example at home. Get a chair and you stand up on top of the chair's set, then have a person (still standing on the floor) take your hand. Now try to pull them up on the chair with you with only your own strength. Once you have failed at doing that, then ask the person standing on the floor below you, ask them to pull you down. Do you see how much easier it is for them to pull you down than for you to pull them up?

That's what will happen daily if you keep those bad influences around you while you are trying to get your peace and happiness degree.

After you have graduated from GOD/JESUS University, which I'd say will take you a minimum of four years living as a solid Christian, then if you still want to go back and help past acquaintances, you will be prepared to handle it, but take a fellow "practicing" Christian with you. Never go alone without a full-fledged older Christian whom has had their GOD/JESUS degree/relationship for many, many years.

Throughout my University of GOD/JESUS education there were times when I became so angry with GOD/JESUS, that one time I ripped up my first Message Bible into pieces while screaming at GOD/JESUS. My daughter had just called again telling me she had been beaten up by one of her male cousins for having told me about him molesting her. When I called police and Child Protective Services, it had gotten that seventeen-year-old boy (my daughter was only nine years old) in a lot of trouble, so when he saw my daughter again, he took revenge.

Talk about feeling helpless, and the worst thing was I could not go to my daughter or I would be arrested; due to all the other times I had tried to defend her, when police and Child Protection were taking months to make a move (through court proceedings). Due to years of previous times I'd tried to defend her myself, her father financially secured a restraining order on me. All the while, my child was left in one dangerous situation after another. Can you imagine my choices every time my child called with accusations of abuse?

1) Go running to protect my daughter and then be thrown in jail AGAIN! or 2) Just sit there, listening to my daughter begging me to help her, listening to the tears and descriptions of horror being bestowed upon my baby. Those were my only choices, that's what it had all boiled down to near the time I finally collapsed with the perforated stomach ulcer. Is it any wonder I developed such heavy narcotic, alcohol & cigarette addictions, near the end of that living hell? Those things are all I had to temporarily stop my heart ache & mental torture.

I get seriously angry just writing about it, however, I must maintain control because getting upset is what satan the hacker wants. That is why I take a deep breath and pull on GOD/JESUS' Wi-Fi (HOLY SPIRIT) connection. Because I have obtained my degree from HIM, I understand what is happening in the spiritual realm. I know, for a fact, all those people who harmed my child and tormented me, they are all now reaping what they had sown. Their lives are all so absolutely wretchedly miserable, yet I did nothing to them, they did it to themselves.

Romans 12:19 (NIV)
> *"Do not take revenge my dear friends, but leave room for GOD's wrath, for it is written: 'It is mine to avenge; I will repay,' says the LORD."*

Deuteronomy 32:34–35 (MSG)
> *"Don't you realize that I have my shelves well stocked, locked behind iron doors? I'M in charge of vengeance and payback, just waiting for them to slip up; and the day of their doom is just around the corner, sudden and swift and sure!"*

Yes, it does sometimes take years for these bad people to get what they gave, nonetheless, it all catches up with them much, much worse than their original sins.

Proverbs 6:31 (NIV)
> *"Yet if he is caught, he must pay sevenfold though it costs him all the wealth of his house."*

This is only one of the many benefits included in GOD/JESUS' cyber protection plan and it is absolutely free!

Back to your peace and happiness degree. Before I get too far into promises of peace and happiness, you must understand that just because you graduate from GOD/JESUS' University, this does not guarantee there won't be any more troubles in life. As a matter of fact, when you first start your Christian life, your problems may increase because satan has had you under his control (in some way or another) for so long that he will not be willing to let you go so easily. He is going to try to make your life seem worse for having tried to go to GOD/JESUS. Just like breaking up from a very destructive relationship, where you want out, but the other person is just fine the way things are. There will be resistance to the breakup. Like a bitter ex trying everything they can to make your life (without them) miserable. The devil will be trying the same childish games. If you will stick with GOD/JESUS' Wi-Fi through the rough patches (like I did) no matter what happens (even brutally holding your child hostage), then you will eventually start to see a new sun rising in your future.

Once you finally achieve the very real sense of a calm, atmospheric-globe surrounding you at all times, then when satan does throw a fireball at you, it will not have the impact that it once did. You will still face problems throughout your life, even as a Christian. However, your reaction will be totally different, you will amaze yourself and, given time, GOD/JESUS will work it all out to your benefit. In the end, GOD/JESUS will flip those attacks right back to where it came from, on top of satan's head! And for you, something good will eventually come out of those bad experiences given enough time. GOD/JESUS can sum it up very nicely for you through:

Deuteronomy 30:1–14 (MSG)
> *"Here's what will happen. While you're out among the nations where GOD has dispersed you and the blessings and curses come in just the way I have set them before you, and your children take them seriously and come back to GOD, and obey HIM with your whole heart and*

soul according to everything that I command you today, GOD, your GOD, will restore everything you lost; HE will have compassion on you; HE will come back and pick up the pieces from all the places where you were scattered. No matter how far away you end up, GOD, your GOD, will get you out of there and bring you back to the land your ancestors once possessed. It will be yours again. HE will give you a good life and make you more numerous than your ancestors. GOD, your GOD, will cut away the thick calluses on your heart and your children's hearts, freeing you to love GOD, your GOD, with your whole heart and soul and live, really live. GOD, your GOD, will put all these curses on your enemies who hated you and were out to get you. And you will make a new start, listening obediently to GOD, keeping all HIS commandments that I'm commanding you today. GOD, your GOD, will outdo HIMSELF in making things go well for you: you'll have babies, get calves, grow crops, and enjoy an all-around good life. Yes, GOD will start enjoying you again, making things go well for you just as HE enjoyed doing it for your ancestors. But only if you listen obediently to GOD, your GOD, and keep the commandments and regulations written in this Book of Revelation. Nothing half-hearted here; you must return to GOD, your GOD, totally, heart and soul, holding nothing back. This commandment that I'm commanding you today isn't too much for you, it's not out of your reach. It's not a high mountain – you don't have to get mountaineers to climb the peak and bring it down to your level and explain it before you can live it. And it's not across the ocean—you don't have to send sailors out to get it, bring it back, and then explain it before you can live it. No. The WORD is right here and now— as near as the heart in your chest. JUST DO IT!"

Since my decision to live the remainder of my life celibate, I have grown so much closer to GOD/JESUS that I no longer feel the need for a marital companion. GOD/JESUS has brought me to a place of such peace, happiness, joy, and love, that I simply could not imagine an actual man who would be able to compete with the relationship I already have with my CREATOR. I love working for GOD/JESUS and in return, HE takes care of me and loves me without arguments, abuse or any controversy whatsoever as long as I am very careful to listen for HIM every day.

Philippians 4:7 (ESV)
"And the peace of GOD, which surpasses all understanding, will guard your hearts and your minds in CHRIST JESUS."

I cannot go back to the life I had known before, where I depended on a human for my happiness. I am not suggesting anyone to live the same, permanently celibate life as myself. All I am saying here is that you must find your happiness with GOD/JESUS first (peace and happiness first), before you become involved with anyone else. If you do not, then you will be depending on your relationship 100 percent to make you happy and solve your every problem. No one can stand up to that kind of pressure, man or woman, we are all struggling through this world. It is hard enough to deal with everyday life and our own problems, but when you hook up with someone and place all your problems on top of their own, then you are rapidly cruising for a bruising. No one relationship can survive by placing all your dependency for happiness on one mortal human being. It's impossible, that's why so many are constantly changing partners but to no avail! Only GOD/JESUS can give that kind of contentment. Put GOD/JESUS in the center of your relationship with someone, then and only then do you have a chance at happiness within a human relationship which can stand the test of time.

Remember how all of those invisible powers each have their own laws and rules? So then does GOD/JESUS in HIS commandments and laws (only for our benefit). Remembering if you do not abide by earth's invisible laws there will be severe consequences. Not because, say gravity for instance, hates you, but because the laws of gravity are the very essence of gravity. Gravity would not be gravity without its laws, and so it goes with all other invisible powers, even GOD/JESUS—especially GOD/JESUS! All those laws are for our benefit, that's the entire purpose of them all!

We must all respect the laws of nature, the laws of the universe, the laws of aerodynamics, hydrodynamics, gravity, and all the rest of the invisible, yet very real laws. We don't consider following those laws to be harsh or uncool, it is simply a given that we either follow those laws or we will suffer greatly, and that is that. So why are GOD/JESUS' laws any different? Why can we not understand that HIS laws are just as important to adhere to in order to avoid suffering? GOD/JESUS is invisible, so what? Gravity is as well and so is your computer's Wi-Fi. Why would we think that GOD/JESUS is not really there simply because we cannot see HIM? We don't doubt gravity, oxygen, the wind power, or Wi-Fi is really there, just because we cannot see it. Just try not obeying the laws of gravity, go jump off a hundred-story building and see what happens! On your way down, right before you die, there will be absolutely no doubt that gravity is real (even though it is invisible). Its laws are just as real as it is. In the same way, GOD/JESUS' laws are for our benefit, to protect us from falling into hell on earth and after death, just like gravity's laws are there to benefit us by keeping us on the ground, as long as we obey its rules, of course. Now this is not to say that we are capable of living "perfect" lives in keeping all Ten Commandments, after all, that's why GOD/JESUS willingly sacrificed HIMSELF on earth. What I am saying is the more effort we put into trying to do right then the less effort we will have to put enduring the suffering caused by knowingly breaking laws, be it natural earthly laws (like gravity) or GOD/JESUS' laws, The Ten Commandments a.k.a "Recommendations For Better Living". GOD/JESUS created HIS rules first and foremost because HE truly, truly LOVES us all and was attempting to spare us all from pain & suffering. Remember those crime/murder shows, remember all that pain, suffering, prison time, murder and death can all be connected to

Breaking GOD/JESUS' Commandments, "The Recommendations For Better Living".

Here's what it's like to say you are a Christian but you don't actually make a conscious and intentional connection to GOD/JESUS' Wi-Fi every day. You know the power invisible oxygen has on the body—just walking around breathing oxygen is normal, then compare 100 percent pure prescription (hospital grade) oxygen, it is so pure it makes you feel like Superman—problems or not, you feel good. That is the difference in going through life with or without a daily conscious and intentional connection with GOD/JESUS. You can still function without HIS connection, which is like daily street oxygen, or you can make that intentionally conscious connection every day, which is like that 100 percent pure prescription oxygen. Problems or not, you can handle it. How can you feel good even with a problem? Because you have a deep seeded knowledge that you are covered by GOD/JESUS' protection and so, like *Jumanji* (1995), you know that no matter what happens, everything will end up absolutely perfect when we finally finish our game/life on our arrival in heaven. In other words, everything happening here on Earth is all very temporary. Also remember to look at your problems like puzzles or teaching tools in that once you solve a problem then you have been taught one more lesson. Every time I am faced with a problem, temptation, or troubling situation, I see it as GOD/JESUS trying to teach me or test me in something. Either way the outcome is for my growth and benefit in the ultimate end. Keep your eyes open for temptation tests because only when you can overcome each obstacle (temptation test) is when GOD/JESUS can and will trust you with more blessings in your life—better job positions, better financial stability, better housing, etc. The basic situation is that when

GOD/JESUS can trust you with small things, then HE knows HE can trust you with a bit more and a bit more and so it goes. When working with GOD/JESUS through life, you will gain with HIM, though ever be it, slowly, little by little. However slowly you may be gaining things through GOD/JESUS' lessons, those things will be with you long term when gained through perseverance with HIM verses gaining things in life rapidly (without HIM) which are lost just as quickly.

The last thing I want to tell you in this chapter is a little story I'd heard from Pastor Joel Osteen on Trinity Broadcasting Network. It's about how you can't please everybody all of the time, which are obstacles you will run into as you start trying to leave bad influences and correct your life.

Our tale begins with an old man, his grandson, and a little donkey (back in Biblical days) who were traveling to Jerusalem to celebrate Passover. The old man was riding the little donkey while the boy walked along side. As they were passing through the first town, they heard someone say, "look at that grown man riding while that poor little boy walks!" So, the grandpa put the little boy on the donkey and he walked. Soon they were passing another town and heard someone saying, "look at that boy riding while the poor, old man walks!" So, they both got on the donkey and continued to the next town where they heard, "look at those two abusing that poor little donkey!" When they finally arrived in Jerusalem, they heard someone saying, "look at those two crazy people carrying their donkey!"

This is a great example of how people can see the very same thing but completely misinterpret what is going on. This same thing will probably happen to you once you change your life and start living and learning everything about GOD/JESUS. Don't worry about what people think because you will never be able to please everyone all the time. You just keep your eyes on GOD/JESUS and try to please HIM and when you do make a mistake then HIS sacrificial death will be there absorbing your sin and covering you in Grace.

In summary of this chapter, please, please, understand what I am trying to say. That is if you will focus completely on learning all about GOD/JESUS, just really get every part of your daily life focused on what GOD/JESUS would do in each daily situation you face. PUT GOD/JESUS FIRST & FOREMOST IN EVERYTHING YOU DO! You WILL see eventually everything with in your life slowly but surely seems to fall into place. That is exactly what happened to me. What has finally happened to me is promised to all with in The Bible verse which follows:

Matthew 6:33 (NIV)
But seek FIRST HIS kingdom and HIS righteousness, and all these things (your daily needs) will be given to you as well.

Keep in mind GOD/JESUS is saying HE will give you your daily NEEDS not your daily GREEDS! Once you get your life finally straightened out enough then you yourself can go for things other than real necessities and you may find GOD/JESUS will surprise you every so often. I want to also show you a more descriptive form of that verse from my all time favorite Bible, The Message Bible which is as follows:

Matthew 6:30-34 (MSG)

> *30 – 33 "If GOD gives such attention to the appearance of wildflowers – most of which are never even seen – don't you think HE will attend to you, take pride in you, do HIS best for you? What I'm trying to do here is to get you to relax, to not be so preoccupied with "getting", so you can respond to GOD's "giving". People who don't know GOD and the way HE works fuss over these things, but you know both GOD and how HE works. Steep your life in GOD – provisions. Don't worry about missing out. You'll find all your every day human concerns will be met." 34. "Give your entire attention to what GOD is doing right now, and don't get worked up about what may or may not happen tomorrow. GOD will help you deal with whatever hard things come up when the time comes."*

In a closing note of this chapter, I want to make something very clear to everyone. We cannot be saved by the things we do good. No one can live a perfect and sinless life (except JESUS). I am not saying to go be perfect or live by only good deeds and perfection because that is impossible. All I am trying to say is simply pay attention and do your best then GOD/JESUS will pick up the slack if you call on HIS NAME.

CHAPTER 12

GOD'S GREAT BEAUTY

My thoughts on this subject are what keeps me celibate in order to focus 100 percent on working for GOD/JESUS and because no man could ever compare to my vision of the ONE I love. When I envision my FATHER in heaven, I see all the most beautiful people in the world who have ever lived, all rolled into one being. Yet that one being is still only a flake of dandruff off of GOD/JESUS' head. Imagine your favorite celebrities and the people you have had serious crushes on. All of the most beautiful and handsome people that have ever caught your attention, then put them all together into one person. One person who has every quality that is absolutely irresistible to you. From beauty to intelligence to personality and wit, that would still only be a fingernail clipping of GOD/JESUS!

After all, we are each made in HIS Image, so it stands to reason that mankind is only a black and white negative of what GOD/JESUS is. HE is the full color photograph framed in gold!

About HIS personality, GOD/JESUS has the most, HIS

intellectually funny wit is unsurpassed. Think of the most intelligent and funny person you know, someone who just cracks you up so bad that you cry while you are laughing, then times that by trillions and you might get a glimpse of GOD/JESUS' funny side! HE displays some of HIS funny wit in the form of the bumblebee, which has confused scientist forever, because it defies the natural laws of physics and aerodynamics. Its tiny, thin, frail wings should not be able to carry its huge, over-proportioned body, yet it flies all over the place, high and low, like nobody's business. I can just almost hear GOD/JESUS snickering right now, too cute!

The duck billed platypus is another enigma which confuses the heck out of mankind. When people first discovered this animal, they thought it was a hoax animal stitched together, kind of like how jackalopes were created as a hoax by attaching antelope horns on a big, jack rabbit. The platypus has a bill like a duck, a tail like a beaver, and the feet of an otter. It lays eggs which are lizard-like, and shoots poison out of its feet, and it is the sole living representative of its family. Talk about a sense of humor, those two animals alone are awesome practical jokes on mankind. Now you know HE's up in heaven just snickering at all of our loss of words to explain those creatures.

My personal favorite enigma within the animal kingdom is the okapi, which looks like GOD/JESUS took a zebra and a giraffe and then mixed it all together.

GOD/JESUS' sense of humor is where we get ours from. If we get our sense of humor from HIM, then it stands to reason that HIS is much more entertaining than humanity's. Just look at cats, I mean seriously! Cats are the ultimate example of GOD/JESUS' sense of sarcastic, witty, intelligent humor. Take a moment to just think about the sense of humor it took to come up with creating a cat's personality!

You know, HE is not all gloom and doom, all serious, all the time. HE is the ultimate practical joker once you get to know about HIM. HE's a flat-out trip!

GOD/JESUS' intelligence has been discussed throughout this book and is displayed worldwide and throughout the universe. I think you already have a pretty good understanding on that subject, though I have only presented a glimpse of what HE truly is. GOD/JESUS is the epitome of supreme knowledge, how else could HE come up with everything in the entire universe?

Here's a good way to understand GOD/JESUS as the creator of all: think about this, when man creates or invents something like a car, jet, computer, even a movie; the one who created said item is not stuck inside that item they created, are they?

Neither then is GOD/JESUS stuck inside our time and space. HE is above and outside of all HIS creation and the universe.

GOD/JESUS presented HIMSELF to Moses and here is how that went.

Exodus 33:18–23 (MSG)

> *"Moses said, 'Please. Let me see your Glory.' GOD said, 'I will make my Goodness pass right in front of you; I'll call out the name, GOD, right before you. I'll treat well whomever I want to treat well and I'll be kind to whomever I want to be kind. But you may not see MY Face. No one can see ME and live. Look, here is a place right beside ME. Put yourself on this rock.*

> *When MY Glory passes by, I'll put you in the cleft of the rock and cover you with MY Hand until I've passed by. Then I'll take MY Hand away and you'll see MY Back. But you won't see my face."*

The result of just this quick passing by of GOD/JESUS' beauty is in the following verse.

Exodus 34:29–30 (MSG)
> *"When Moses came down from Mt. Sinai carrying the two Tablets of The Testimony, he didn't know that the skin of his face glowed because he had been speaking with GOD. Aaron and all the Israelites saw Moses, saw his radiant face, and held back, afraid to get close to him."*

Think about this, have you ever seen one of those centuries-old, huge, man-sized, beautiful vases? Now have you ever seen one of those vases which is a beautiful mosaic (broken pieces put back together)? Those are a great analogy for GOD/JESUS. GOD is the smooth, perfect, life-sized, centuries-old vase, while JESUS is the same vase only broken and put back together as a mosaic!

What follows is an example of the Beauty GOD/JESUS will bestow upon your life from time to time if you will stay connected daily to HIS Wi-Fi. Once I got hooked up to HIS Wi-Fi and my life began to smooth out, I was experiencing an unusually bad day when all of a sudden I heard "Julie, Julie, (my name) you are beautiful beyond words, altogether beautiful, come with me, you have captured my heart, you hold it hostage with one glance, your love delights me......."! I heard this coming from my living room, I almost feel out. I walked in my living room and there on my T.V. was actor Clark Gable (1901-1960) speaking those words to a girl named "Julie" in the film "Strange Cargo" (1940). He was speaking words from The Bible, Song Of Songs 4:1-11. Now I'm not all-that yet GOD/JESUS sees us all exactly like that. Clark Gable is my all-time favorite actor too, so not only did GOD/JESUS send me an uplifting word but HE did it through my favorite actor! These are the kinds of experiences you can look forward to once connected to GOD/JESUS Wi-Fi.

Last but not least, please be aware that you are not finished with this book and all its proof and knowledge of the INVISIBLE realms until you have watched all suggested film and read all suggested books! The reason being that those things are proof and back up everything discussed within these pages.

THE END

Romans 1:20 (NIV)

"For since the creation of the world GOD's INVISIBLE qualities – HIS eternal power and divine nature – have been clearly seen, being understood from what has been made, so that people are without excuse!"

HOW TO BECOME A CHRISTIAN BY ASKING GOD/JESUS INTO YOUR LIFE: Go to the internet, look up "THE SALVATION POEM-SUPERBOOK." It plays as a song to sing along with or look up the words/lyrics and read them aloud The Salvation Poem - SuperBook is animated, however, it is still perfect for adults too for the reasoning that GOD/JESUS wants each of us to come to HIM as little children. That's it—once you have spoken those words, you have asked GOD/JESUS into your life, now that you are a Christian, find a Church to become involved with. Also, you may request a totally free "New-Christian" packet from The Christian Broadcasting Network by calling 1-800-700-7000, these people are available 24/7 & will pray with you or even walk you through your own request to GOD/JESUS for salvation of your soul. They can also answer any questions you may have on establishing a new relationship with GOD/JESUS. They will do all of the above, absolutely free of any cost or obligation whatsoever.

WARNINGS FOR NEW CHRISTIANS

1. Be careful when looking for a new church. Meaning that there are organizations out there that use JESUS' and other forms of GOD's name to confuse people, but they do not believe GOD/JESUS to be our only SAVIOR. A good rule of thumb is to watch TBN (Trinity Broadcasting Network) Christian TV until you clearly understand what a true Christian Church is, then pick out a pastor you like, look up their denomination (or non-denomination), then search for a church in your area with that same affiliation. The hacker satan, is always out in front of new Christians, trying to trip them up anyway possible, so be aware of how subtle the devil can be.

    I am a member of a non-denominational church. However, when I'm traveling, I like to go to some of the other denominations from TBN, so that I can experience the entire body of the church, and they are fun and informative as well.

2. Beware of playing with spirit calling, seance boards, or witchcraft, even if it says it is good witchcraft, that is an oxymoron. You will

actually be working with demons in doing spells and talking to spirits, not loved ones or GOD/JESUS' angels.

The same goes for seances, if you do bring in any spirit, it is guaranteed to be a demon. They may seem like a harmless relative or helpful spirit at first, but in the end, it will completely destroy your life. If you think you want to try any of these things because your desperate to solve a serious problem; let me tell you, after those demons are finished with you, you will think the original problem you had was a fairy tale compared to the numerous problems you will have after becoming involved with spirits! Unless you just have a craving for extra-hellish problems, then stay away from all forms of this!

3. Be careful of the words you speak, remembering that GOD/JESUS, HIMSELF had to speak to bring things into existence. Within the beginning of every verse where GOD/JESUS creates something it states, "Then GOD said, Let there be. . . ." If GOD/JESUS, HIMSELF had to speak things into being then you must comprehend that when a human being repeatedly speaks of something, it can be spoken into fruition eventually so be careful of the words you speak and songs you sing along with! The following are the times GOD/JESUS spoke things into existence:

Genesis 1:3 (NLT) "Then GOD SAID, 'Let there be light, and there was light.'"

Genesis 1:6-7 (NLT) 6. "Then GOD SAID, 'Let there be a space between the waters, to separate the waters of the heavens from the waters of the earth.'" 7. "And that is what happened . . ."

Genesis 1:9 (NLT) "Then GOD SAID, 'Let the waters beneath the sky flow together into one place, so dry ground may appear.' And that is what happened."

Genesis 1:11 (NLT) "Then GOD SAID, 'Let the land sprout with vegetation – every sort of seed-bearing fruit. These seeds will then produce the kinds of plants and trees from which they came.' And that is what happened."

Genesis 1:14 (NLT) "Then GOD SAID, 'Let lights appear in the sky to separate the day from the night. Let them be signs to mark the seasons, days, and years.'"

Genesis 1:20 (NLT) "Then GOD SAID, 'Let the waters swarm with fish and other life. Let the skies be filled with birds of every kind.'"

Genesis 1:24 (NLT) "Then GOD SAID, 'Let the earth produce every sort of animal, each producing offspring of the same kind – livestock, small animals that scurry along the ground, and wild animals.' And that is what happened."

Genesis 1:26 (NLT) "Then GOD SAID, 'Let US make human beings in our image, to be like US. They will reign over the fish in the sea, the birds in the sky, the livestock, all the wild animals on the earth, and the small animals that scurry along the ground.'"

If you are constantly speaking bad about yourself like, "I'm so dumb," "I have the worst luck," or "I'm so ugly," "I will never get better or regain my health," you will eventually speak them into reality. Invisible words are powerful, so be very careful what you say about yourself, your children, family, and friends. Be careful when you are listening to music and singing along with a song, you are speaking the words of that song out loud. If it is foul music speaking of murder, drugs and addiction, prostitution, etc., then you are speaking those things into your life. Please be careful. Do not allow your flesh (urges) to rule your life, GOD/JESUS and you are the only ones who should be controlling your daily actions and the words you speak.

PROVERBS 18:21 (MSG) "Words kill, words give life; they're either poison or fruit – you choose!"

4. Be forewarned, you absolutely, unequivocally, must, must, must have complete and total forgiveness in your heart for everyone who has ever harmed you. Unforgiveness of others is a complete blocker, preventing GOD/JESUS from giving you all the forgiveness you yourself need. If HE can't fully forgive you then HE can't fully bless your life with

answered pray, etc. (Listen, if I can forgive those who harmed my daughter and myself, then I know you can forgive people too.) I do not mean go befriend your enemy, just simply forgive them within your heart.

5. Stop complaining! Do not complain about everything. Be grateful, there's always someone worse off than you. If you are in the situation I was in (where nothing can make you grateful) then at least do not continue to complain. Speak when you must to whomever you must, professionally to discuss your situation and then be quiet outside of that (give it to GOD/JESUS at all other times). Only when we stop complaining is when GOD/JESUS will start moving in your life.

6. Last but not least, GOD/JESUS will forgive you for absolutely anything (even murder). The only one thing HE cannot forgive is NOT accepting HIS sacrifice on the cross!

GOD/JESUS loves you endlessly & eternally even with our sins as long as we are ever trying to correct them and repent! GOD/JESUS LOVES YOU!!!!!!!

MOVIES EVERY NEW CHRISTIAN MUST SEE

(They are not in any viewing order except for # 1. "HEAVEN", this should be seen first.)

1. Heaven: What God Has Prepared for Those Who Love Him (2016) Documentary by Pat Robertson
2. The Apocalypse (2002) Lead Actor: Richard Harris/Feature Film
3. Faith Like Potatoes (2006) Frank Rautenbach Film/Documentary
4. Machine Gun Preacher (2011) Gerard Butler Film/Documentary
5. War Room (2015) T.C. Stallings, Priscilla Shirer/Feature Film
6. Heaven is For Real (2014) Greg Kinnear, Kelly Reilly Film/Documentary
7. GOD's Not Dead (2014), GOD's Not Dead 2 (2016), and GOD's Not Dead: A Light in Darkness (2018)
8. SuperBook: In the Beginning (2011) Animated (for adults as well) CBN Productions
9. The Harbinger Decoded (2013) by Johnathan Cahn Documentary Film

10. Against All Odds: Israel Survives (2006) Miraculous True Stories Feature-length-film Documentary/Movie. This film has interviews with Muslim militants who were involved in the Israeli wars of 1947 through 1970s, these enemies of Israel claim to have seen giant (over seven ft. tall) Israeli soldier's numbered in the thousands, which caused them to run from Israel. However, it is a historical fact that Israel only had a few hundred men at best during the times of these sightings and they were most certainly not over seven feet tall. The conclusion on both sides of the conflict is that GOD/JESUS had sent HIS very army from heaven to stop the fighting. This documentary will astound you!
11. The Shack (2017) Sam Worthington, Octavia Spencer/Feature Film
12. The Perfect Gift (2009) Christina Fougnie/Feature Film
13. Revive Us and Revive Us 2 (2016) by Kirk Cameron/Documentary Film
14. Visions of The Night: How God Speaks in Dreams (2014) by Gordon Robertson/Documentary Film
15. The Tithe Project (2017) The Film/Documentary. This has very important financial direction on how a Christian should handle money.
16. The Case for Christ (2017) Lee Strobel (former atheist) Feature Film/Documentary

17. Pilgrim's Progress (2019) John Rhys-Davies (Animated for adults and children) Feature Film
18. Day of Discovery: "The Time to Live Is Now: Legacy of Lygon Stevens" (2013) Documentary.
19. To Life: How Israeli Volunteers are Changing the World (2018) Gordon Robertson/ Documentary
20. HEAVEN (DVD) BillyGrahamBookstore.org
21. Made in Israel (2013) Documentary by Gordon Robertson CBN Productions
22. Written in Stone Documentary Series Gordon Robertson CBN Productions

WEEKLY SHOWS TO WATCH

1. "Creation in the 21st Century" (series) David Rives
2. "The Way of The Master" (series) Ray Comfort and Kirk Cameron
3. "The 700 Club" by Christian Broadcasting Network CBN (daily)
4. "CBN News Channel" 24/7 Christian Perspective News
5. Trinity Broadcasting Networks TBN Christian TV (24/7-daily/nightly)
6. "BILLYGRAHAM.TV" Franklin Graham on-going Series
7. "FINDPEACEWITHGOD.TV"

MUST-READ BOOKS

1. *Akiane: Her Life, Her Art, Her Poetry* (2006)
   This is a forty-page biography about a little girl named Akiane (written from the pages of her mother's diary). From an atheistic family, Akiane started painting at the age of five years old. She says GOD/JESUS taught her how and I believe her; you will, too, once you see them and hear her story. She has been on Oprah, CNN, FOX News and many, many other shows. This book is full of Akiane's poetry (which has astounded scholar's from around the world) and of her most popular color paintings selling in the high six figures, which goes to charity.

2. *The Blessed Life: Unlocking the Rewards of Generous Living* and *Beyond Blessed: God's Perfect Plan to Overcome All Financial Stress.* Both are written by Pastor Robert Morris
   These books are extremely important when starting a new Christian lifestyle. It will direct you on how GOD/JESUS expects you to handle your money. It explains how to get financially organized as a Christian so that, indeed, you will have a very "Blessed Life." It has been so successful in helping people with their

finances that it has been printed in forty different languages all around the world!

3. *Answers to Prayer* by George Mueller (1805-1898)

    Must read *The Blessed Life* books by Robert Morris first, in order to understand this book. This man opened many orphanages and supported them all financially by prayer alone! He documented all his financial troubles and needs, and then how GOD/JESUS miraculously supplied every need for over fifty years! The stories he wrote will blow your mind and build your faith.

4. *GODs Influence in The Making of America* by Donald S. Conkey and published by BookLogix.

DIRECTION FOR LIFE'S CHALLENGE'S

FOR MOLESTATION VICTIMS:

To anyone who has endured sexual molestation or incest once or for years, please start watching *JOYCE MEYER*. See her testimony on the internet. Her father raped her as a small child, until she was old enough to leave home. Her redemption story and testimony can absolutely change your life. She also helps world-wide recovery of sex traffic victims along with several other Women's Recovery organizations. There is much hope for you!

JOYCE MEYER MINISTRIES
P.O. BOX 655
FENTON, MO. 63026
1-866-480-1528
www.joycemeyer.org

FOR GANGSTERS:

Look up *MICHAEL FRANZESE*, former American crime boss out of New York. This man survived leaving the mob, and tells incredible stories in his speaking events, books, and his true-life story, *"From the Godfather to God the Father: The Michael Francise Story."* There is much hope for you!

NICKY CRUZ (another former gangster) was raised in Puerto Rico in a satanic/ witchcraft family who severely tortured him daily. At fifteen, he moved to New York and became the leader of the most murderous gang there, the MAU MAUS. Confronted by a street Preacher, he threatened to murder him. Nicky now works with serious gangsters turning them to CHRIST JESUS through:

NICKY CRUZ OUTREACH

Please watch *Nicky Cruz* interviews/testimony via the internet.

FOR SATAN WORSHIPPERS AND WITCHCRAFT:

See books, interviews, and film on *JOHN RAMIREZ*, former top-satan cult leader, who discovered GOD/JESUS' power always defeated satan's power when he was a practicing satanist. There is much hope for you!

FOR SERIOUS DRUG ADDICTS:

Look up *Mike Lindell, the My Pillow guy*. He was a serious crack addict for more than a decade who, after having a GOD/JESUS-given dream, created *My Pillow*. Now he uses the money to open and fund Christian drug recovery centers. His book is *What Are the Odds? From Crack Addict to CEO by Mike J. Lindell*. This guy ended up in the White House, befriending the president of the free world! There's a hologram picture of Mike on the front of his book, it's a picture of him that his dealer took after smoking crack for two weeks straight. There is much hope for you!

FOR THE HANDICAPPED:

Please look up *Australian Evangelist NICK VUJICIC* who was born without any legs or arms at all. Nick travels the world speaking to the hope and saving grace which GOD/JESUS gave him and can give you as well. He is extremely encouraging and uplifting. Nick's testimony (life story) may be viewed on many different web sites via the internet. If you are handicapped, there is much hope for you!

FOR PTS MILITARY:

Please see DAVE ROEVER's life story. He has several books about all he endured (and continues to endure) from his experience in war. A grenade exploded beside his head and absolutely disfigured him. He has made a spiritual recovery though you can still see the physical affects all over his body. Dave Roever is Founder, Chairman, and President of two non-profit corporations: ROEVER EVANGELISTIC ASSOCIATION and ROEVER EDUCATIONAL ASSISTANCE PROGRAMS. There is much hope for you!

ROEVER FOUNDATION
P.O. Box 136130
Fort Worth , Texas 76136
1-817-238-2000
info@roeverfoundation.org

FOR THE BREATHING HUMAN:

There is much hope for you all! Please see THE CROSS: BILLY GRAHAM TV SPECIAL documentary (28 minutes free on Youtube), interviews of many different troubled lives. HEAVEN: A NEW MESSAGE FROM BILLY GRAHAM is another 28-minute documentary which may be viewed for free on the internet via several different websites. This video is one of my favorites. I keep a stock of the DVDs to give out in the streets on my daily errands. They may be purchased at **BILLYGRAHAMBOOKSTORE.com**

ABOUT HUMAN/CHILD SEX TRAFFICKING:

Please educate yourself and others by visiting *"THE A21 CAMPAIGN"* founded (2008) by *Christine Caine*. This is a world-wide campaign to stop all forms of human trafficking/slavery (which is alive and very well today). The web page is *www.a21.org* where you can learn what you can do in simply keeping your eyes open and reporting suspicious activity, if not also donating.

If you are a victim of sex trafficking or human-slavery trafficking, please call **THE NATIONAL HUMAN TRAFFICKING HOTLINE** 1-888-373-7888 or email help@humantraffickinghotline.org. There is much hope for you.

SUGGESTED FIRST BIBLE:

The Message Bible by Eugene H. Peterson

This Bible is like everyday street talk, so it is very easy to read. It is The Bible I used most when quoting scripture throughout this book.

PLACES TO VISIT FOR PHYSICAL PROOF OF GOD/JESUS:

#1. MUSEUM OF THE BIBLE

400 4th Street S.W.
Washington, D.C. 20024
1-866-430-6682
Museumofthebible.org

#2. ARK ENCOUNTER & CREATION MUSEUM

1 Ark Encounter Drive
Williamstown, KY. 41097
1-859-727-2222
Arkencounter.com

CLOSING BIBLE VERSE

Psalm 91:14–16 (MSG)
> *"If you'll hold on to ME for dear life, says GOD, I'll get you out of any trouble. I'll give you the best of care if you'll only get to know and trust ME. Call ME and I'll answer, be at your side in bad times; I'll rescue you, then throw you a party. I'll give you a long life, give you a long drink of salvation!"*

FINAL GREETINGS & LAST WORDS TO ENCOURAGE YOU

As I mentioned before, I may well be looking at my own mortality sooner than later. At the moment (March 2022) I am going through major diagnostic work ups by several different specialist to determine what is causing my immune system to severally crash, no one can seem to find the answers. I have been told that I have all the signs of a hidden cancer within me, which they are looking for at the moment. It may be no big deal or it may be the biggest deal. No matter what it is, I DO NOT want you to think that GOD/JESUS failed to heal me if I were to actually pass on. Quite the contrary, if I pass then that means GOD/JESUS has indeed healed me 100% in Heaven. Let me explain this, when we pray and beg GOD/JESUS to heal our loved ones and then they get better, that (earthly) healing is only a 50% healing because we are still on earth in a body (though healed momentarily) continually decaying 24/7. The true healing is only achieved through faith in GOD/JESUS which will deliver us to Heaven upon our death. If you have a loved one you prayed for and they still passed on, your prayers were answered because your loved one was 100% healed upon their arrival to Heaven! Please believe me when I tell you that "death" is not necessarily a bad thing. I have already been there and back so I can tell you, without a doubt, that death is simply a transfer of our souls to a different realm, an **INVISIBLE** realm. The release of the spirit from the physical body is an absolutely wondrous, awesome & freeing experience unless it's by suicide. I have experienced two types of near-death experiences thus far, from surgery/illness death and from attempting suicide. Please know that they are not the same. The instant you leave the body from suicide, you immediately understand that you did not escape your problems. It is explained rapidly that you will still have to endure the problems you were trying to escape. Plus you will have to re-experience everything that brought you to that point all over. This is because GOD/JESUS is trying to give us learning experiences to teach us things which we will greatly need in eternity with HIM. After the suicide experience, I was certainly glad I got to come back, however upon leaving the body due to illness and accidents, I felt more alive than I ever did while inside the flesh body. It's exhilarating, so exciting that you think you will burst with love & joy! I was NOT happy to come back to my body on this account. I begged &

pleaded to stay with GOD/JESUS for a really long time it seemed but I woke up a few days later in my body once again. This made me severally depressed because of how free and happy I had been while out of my body. I tell you all of this for two reasons, one for your own loved ones who have passed and also in the case of my own passing. Like that song I said I would love played at my funeral by MAVERICK CITY MUSIC **"The Story I'll Tell"** (2020), GOD/JESUS did not fail me and (whether dead or alive) I am testifying to that with this book!!!

So please DO NOT lose your faith if I am promoted to Heaven, let it make you stronger so satan does not get a win at any angle. In closing of my last greetings I want you to read what Paul wrote in:

Colossians 2: 1-5 (The Message Bible)

"**(1)** I want you to realize that I continue to work as hard as I know how for you, & also for the Christians over Laodicea. Not many of you have met me face-to-face, but that doesn't make any difference. Know that I'm on your side, right alongside you. You're not in this alone. **(2-4)** I want you woven into a tapestry of love, in touch with everything there is to know of GOD. Then you will have minds confident and at rest, focused on Christ, GOD's great MYSTERY. All the richest treasures of wisdom & knowledge are embedded in that MYSTERY and nowhere else. And we've been shown the MYSTERY! I'm telling you this because I don't want anyone leading you off on some wild-goose chase, after other so-called mysteries, or "the secret".

(5) I'm a long way off, true, and you may never lay eyes on me, but believe me, I'm on your side, right beside you. I am delighted to hear of careful and orderly ways you conduct your affairs, and impressed with the solid substance of your faith in CHRIST.

To GOD/JESUS, I give a song (covered) by Lucy Thomas, "AT LAST" (2021).

To my daughter, I give a song (covered) by Celtic Woman, "Fields of Gold" (2017) Official Live Video.

Acknowledgments

I want to thank THE FATHER, THE SON CHRIST JESUS, and THE HOLY SPIRIT (our babysitter).

Also I want to thank Paul & Jane Crouch for having started TBN.

Last but not least, my favorite Christian speakers:

Pastor *Tony Evans* Thank you!

Protestant Preacher *Francis Chan* Thank you!

Christian Evangelist *Priscilla Shirer* Thank you!

About the Author

I am "The Women at the Well" John 4:4-26.

I am "The Fool Who Confounds the Wise" 1 Corinthians 1:27.

I am a graduate of the school of Hard knocks with more than twenty years' experience in extreme physical and mental suffering.

I am the wisdom in ignorance.

I have been wealthy, homeless, a beautiful actress and model.

I have lost children; I have died several times through medically documented horrific situations.

Living a completely celibate life for the past seven years and dedicated to continuing a celibate life until my departure from this earth.

I am a simple nobody who truly loves all human life and so am attempting to spare as many as possible from all I endured due to my previous lack of knowledge in the INVISIBLE realms.

For a mini-biography on the author see pages 64 – 90.

Available on AMAZON.com